Edmund C. P Hull

Coffee

Its physiology, history, and cultivation - adapted as a work of reference for Ceylon,

Wynaad, Coorg and The Neilgherries

Edmund C. P Hull

Coffee

Its physiology, history, and cultivation - adapted as a work of reference for Ceylon, Wynaad, Coorg and The Neilgherries

ISBN/EAN: 9783337228279

Printed in Europe, USA, Canada, Australia, Japan

Cover: Foto ©Andreas Hilbeck / pixelio.de

More available books at **www.hansebooks.com**

COFFEE;

ITS

PHYSIOLOGY, HISTORY AND CULTIVATION:

ADAPTED AS A WORK OF REFERENCE FOR

CEYLON, WYNAAD, COORG AND THE NEILGHERRIES.

BY

EDMUND C. P. HULL.

Madras:
GANTZ BROTHERS,
ADELPHI PRESS, 175, MOUNT ROAD.
1865.

INTRODUCTION.

In the present time, when so much Capital is being expended on, and so much attention given to, Coffee cultivation, the subject of the present work is one of great importance, and I have been the more tempted to write on it, on taking into consideration the paucity of reliable information bearing on it, which has yet been published.

The only works devoted to Coffee cultivation, with which I am acquainted, are—

    Laborie's Coffee Planter of St. Domingo.
    Abridgment of do. by Higginbotham.
    W. on Pruning.
    Wall on Manuring, and
    Dr. Shortt's Hand-book.

The oldest of these, Laborie's, is an excellent work in its way, but as it was written many years ago, it is not surprising that many improvements should have been introduced into Coffee cultivation since its publication, and, moreover, as it was intended to apply mostly to the cultivation of the plant in the West Indies, it is not a very great assistance to the young planter in the Eastern side of the hemispheres.

W.'s paper on Pruning is most useful as a guide to that particular branch of the subject, and is written by one of the most experienced and intelligent of the Ceylon planters; as it will be seen in the body of the present work, I have been indebted to it for some of my remarks on *Pruning*, assistance which I have much pleasure in acknowledging.

Dr. Shortt's Hand-book contains much that is instructive and interesting in Analyses, Statistics, &c.; its *practical* hints, however, are few and difficult of application; this is not to be wondered at when we read the author's preface, in which Dr. Shortt informs us that he is "merely an amateur planter," and that his "*experiments* extend over a few plants only."

Mr. Wall's paper on *Manuring* is a valuable authority on this branch of cultivation, and will be found useful to every planter, and some hints which I have taken from it will add to the value of my chapter on the same subject.

Thus, I trust, it will be apparent, that a want was felt by the planting community, especially by those who have newly joined it, of a work embracing all subjects connected with coffee planting, which might be made available as an adviser at any moment when difficulty or doubt was experienced.

In bringing the present work before the public, my object has been to make it a vade-mecum to any person, who having a small capital which he desires to increase, and deciding on doing so by means of the produce of the coffee tree, to take in his hand, go and select his land, and carry on every necessary work, with system, regularity, and confidence; this without any previous knowledge of planting, and in situations where it may be impossible to obtain the aid of the experience of others.

With this object in view, I have endeavoured to be as minute and exact in the description of each work, as possible. I have been indebted for much that is useful and practical to Mr. Loudon's work on Gardening, it having occurred to me that many of the operations of culture, practised by scientific gardeners in Europe, might with advantage be applied to the cultivation of coffee in the East.

Some of my Physiological information I have obtained from that beautiful work, Rhind's Vegetable Kingdom, and some from Dr. Willick's Encyclopædia.

Chambers's Encyclopædia also contained some historical facts connected with the subject, which I took the liberty of extracting.

Written, as the present work has been, in the jungle, it was out of my power to obtain the assistance of many books, which I would gladly have repaired to, such as Balfour's Botany, Cyclopædia, &c., but the absence of extensive compilation on the theoretical branches of the subject, tend to make the work more handy and practical, which is of greater importance.

I do not pretend to bring out much that is new on the subject of coffee planting, what I have written being simply the results of my own experience, and of my observation of the operations of others ; nor do I suppose, for an instant, that other planters of the same experience know less on the subject than myself; to them I look for corroboration and support, that beginners may regard the present work, notwithstanding its deficiencies, with confidence as a trustworthy friend and adviser.

At this present time, when the scarcity of labour in India presents so alarming an aspect, it will, unfortunately, be in most cases barely possible to cultivate an estate in the exact method here described, but the object I have endeavoured to keep in view being the manner in which a *model Coffee Estate ought* to be conducted, I believe I may confidently advise as close an adherence to the rules I have laid down, as possible.

Like all questions of supply and demand, however, that of labour will eventually right itself, and I have no doubt that the first symptom of improvement will be when our Government begins to regard the interests and welfare of the Peninsula as of greater importance than that of the West Indies, Mauritius,

Natal, and countries the property of other nations, to which, year after year, they permit the exportation of the thews and sinews of the land : it being worthy of notice that a very small proportion of the labour so exported ever returns.

It is strange that a work, similar to the present one, has not before been undertaken by any other planter; many of whom, I am aware, are better qualified than myself for the undertaking, as, in these days of a copious literature, there are few subjects of so great importance which have not been written about, till they may be said to be exhausted.

Such not being the case, however, I trust the motives which induced me to enter claims for authorship will not be misconstrued, but that my book may meet with a friendly, even though it may receive a severe, criticism.

Close examination of its contents I do not deprecate, but whatever shortcomings and defects are discovered in it will, I trust, be treated with leniency.

Should the present edition receive sufficient encouragement to tempt me to venture on bringing out a second one, such hints and corrections as I may in the meantime receive from my brother-planters, shall receive the fullest consideration, and in this manner I can promise that my second edition will be a more complete and valuable work than the present.

Digitized by the Internet Archive
in 2007 with funding from
Microsoft Corporation

http://www.archive.org/details/coffeeitsphysiol00hullrich

INDEX.

CHAPTER I.

Page.

COFFEE BOTANICALLY AND PHYSIOLOGICALLY CONSIDERED—

Botanical description..	1
When first introduced to the notice of Europeans............	3
Nutritive and medicinal properties.............................	4
Coffee-houses...	6
Coffee-tea...	7
Analysis of coffee..	9

CHAPTER II.

Some account of Ceylon, Wynaad, Coorg, the Neilgherries, Mysore, and the Shevaroys, as coffee-producing districts—

Introduction into Ceylon...	14
Kandy...	17
Coffee Districts of Ceylon.......................................	18
Labour in Ceylon...	20
WYNAAD, description of...	21
Labour in Wynaad...	22
Necessity for combination amongst planters....................	24
Steps to be taken to introduce Labour into Wynaad............	25
THE NEILGHERRIES, Ootacamund, Labour...........................	29
MYSORE AND MUNZERABAD, COORG, Mercara.........................	30
SHEVAROY HILLS...	32

CHAPTER III.

Terms for, and means of procuring suitable land in Ceylon and Southern India—

	Page.
Ceylon...	33
In Wynaad...	34
In Coorg..	35

CHAPTER IV.

Elevation, lay, site, temperature, aspect and soils—temperature and elevation..	37
Necessity for humidity of atmosphere........................	39
Small yield at great elevation....................................	40
South-west Monsoon..	41
Site, evils of an exposed situation, Wind...................	42
Northern and Eastern fencings best...........................	46
Lay...	46

CHAPTER V.

Soil...	50
Plants, the most certain indicators of........................	51
Necessity for absorbent power in hot climates..........	52
Stagnant water injurious to all land plants................	53

CHAPTER VI.

Opening—Coolies—Tools—difficulty of getting coolies...	54
Advance system...	55
Mountaineers, and hill tribes preferable—Labour.....	59
Tools..	59
Billhooks..	60
Axes, crowbars, quintannies, &c..............................	61
Care in selecting site for cooly lines.........................	62
The Bamboo..	63
Temporary Bungalow...	64

	Page.
CHAPTER VII.	
Nurseries—Jungle plants in Ceylon	65
Time of year to commence work	66
Seeds—and seed beds and sowing	66
Description of germinating process	67
Dr. Shortt's work	67
Evil of watering during sunshine	68
CHAPTER VIII.	
Felling and clearing	71
Felling Bamboos	72
Lopping, Firing	73
Jungle Leeches	75
CHAPTER IX.	
Lining, Pitting and Filling	76
Lining squares—the West Indies, Java	77
Distances between rows	78
Quincunxes, Pitting or Holing, not less than $1\frac{1}{2}$ feet	79
Contracts for Pitting, Filling in	81
CHAPTER X.	
Planting, Stumps, pruning the roots	83
Planting with ball—method of planting	84
Puddling	85
Age and size of plants	86
Hanging the plants	87
Dibbling	88
CHAPTER XI.	
Roads, Draining, Resume	91
Roads	92
Patent road tracer—tracing	93
Blasting	95
Draining—surface draining on slopes	96

	Page.
Easy gradients—Mr. Wall..	97
Draining swampy ground—Mauritius grass—Grass cutting machine..	98

CHAPTER XII.

Weeding, Filling up vacancies, exhaustive effects of weeds, means of removing weeds..	99
Frequency of weeding—by hand—with the scraper............	100
With the mamootie—Burying in—cost of...........................	101
Filling up vacancies—old trees dying, cause of in old soils...	102

CHAPTER XIII.

Shelter—protection and shade—staking............................	104
European method—shade..	105
Trees acting as a blight—trees exhale noxious gases..........	106
Jack tree—Loquat tree...	107
Trees should not be planted too close together..................	
Mauritius—Castor oil plant..	108
Plantains and bananas...	109

CHAPTER XIV.

Bungalow and Lines..	110
Stone and mortar—Bricks..	111
Tile making—"Wattle and dab"...	114
White ants—trees proof against..	115
Laterite, or cabook—roofs—thatch cadjans—shingles.........	116
Cost of putting on shingles—Tiles—Iron roofs...................	118
Preventing Iron roofs from blowing off..............................	119
Cost of building Bungalows—Floors...................................	121
Sawing timber—Ceylon and Malabar measurement.............	122
Coolie lines—Land wind—necessity of water.....................	123
Cleanliness necessary for health—charpoys—plastering with cowdung—whitewash..	124
Coolies' gardens—liability to combustion...........................	125

CHAPTER XV.

	Page
Topping, Handling, and Pruning	
Topping—height at which necessary—cold climates—exposed situations	126
In sheltered situations—keeping the ground covered—height of a tree not affecting its productiveness	127
Disadvantage of high trees—method of topping	128
Primaries—secondaries	129
Handling—description of form and economy of coffee tree	130
Tertiaries	131
Objects of pruning—method of	132
Criterion of good pruning	133
Systematic handling ensures good pruning	134
Primaries not to be cut	135
Cost of pruning	136

CHAPTER XVI.

	Page
Manuring—object of	137
Plants consist of	138
Substances useful as manure	139
Vegetation green—Woody fibres	
Wood-ashes—Dead bodies—Poonac	140
Bones—Guano—Sal ammoniac	141
Coffee pulp—Thatch grass	142
Cattle dung—Argols	143
Humic acid—proper condition of manure for application—method of preparing manure in German-Switzerland	144
Dr. Shortt's method—method followed in Ceylon	145
Author's method	146
Advantage of proximity to a public road—manner of applying manure with most benefit—not to be put in too deep	147
Cost of manuring	148
Method of application for pulverized manures	149

CHAPTER XVII.

	Page.
Diseases—causes of	150
Bug	151
White Bug	153
Worm	154
Grubs	155
Rats and grasshoppers, their depredations	156

CHAPTER XVIII.

Crop—Description of blossom	157
Picking—Arab method	158
Strong men often bad pickers—Green berries—overripe berries in wet weather—in dry	160
Iron spouting—method of laying—cherry loft	161
Pulping—washing—drying—despatching	162
Uncertainty of weather in Ceylon—not so in Wynaad—Mr. Clerihew's patent	163

CHAPTER XIX.

Stores—Pulping houses and machinery—cherry loft—cisterns	164
Ample supply of water necessary—pulping—pulpers	165
Crusher—Butler's pulper	166
Ceylon planter on pulpers	167
Disc pulper	169
Stores—Iron stores—two-storied stores	170
Fans—ample barbecue room desirable	172
Trays—curing, criterion of good—setting of pulper	173

CHAPTER XX.

Estimates, &c.—outlay in purchase of land	175
Average of cost of—Estimate for Wynaad	176
Condition of estate, and value at end of six years—cost of bringing to that period	185

	Page.
Estimate applicable to Ceylon	186
Difference between the Wynaad and Ceylon estimate—reasons of	192
Dr. Shortt's estimates	193

CHAPTER XXI.

	Page.
Medical hints—medicines required—Fever	200
Bowel complaint—Dysentery	203
Cholera	204
Liver	205
Snake bites	206
Cuts and wounds	207
Fractures and dislocations—Sores	208

DIRECTORY.

NORTH WYNAAD.

Name by which known to Europeans.	Name by which known to Natives.	Names of Proprietors.	Names of Managers.
Alitoor	Haltoor	J. A. Cameron	R. C. Wotherspoon
Agampoora Mulla	Agampoora Mulla	J. M. Closson	J. M. Closson
Bahgoor Mulla	Bahgoor Mulla	P. H. Gordon	J. Gilby
Bellevue	Bullia Mulla	Carneggie and others	W. N. Higinbothom
Bon Accord	Kanatee Mulla	Colonel Smith	A. R. Higinbothom
Bon Espoir	Dindimul	Do.	Do.
Balmoral	Atty Mulla	Beetham	C. F. Wilkins
Bushy Park	Croocherpardy	J. Macfarlane	G. Hubbard
Brahmagherry	Beermagherry	Madras Coffee Co. (Limited.)	John Brown
Bargherry	Bargherry	Limjee Manockjee	J. R. Malcolm
Collessie	Collessie	J. Macfarlane	W. F. Macfarlane
Carticollum	Carticollum	Forman & Steven	J. R. Malcolm
Chapara Mulla	Chapara Mulla	Aiken	C. A. Vernéde
Chenga Moodin	Chenga Moodin Mulla	J. Gordon	W. Gladstone
Coomben Mulla	Coomben Mulla	O'Halloran	L. J. O'Halloran
Canoot Mulla	Canoot Mulla	J. M. Closson	J. M. Closson
Coonda Coon	Coonda Coon	J. A. Cameron	R. C. Wotherspoon
Charlotte	Terrioot	Boyd & Co.	Jeffries
Coondoor	Coondoor	P. H. Gordon	J. W. Smith
Dindimul	Dindamul	Fraser and Dunbar	T. R. Richmond
Drumcree	Dumgherry	Thompson and Richmond	F. E. Richmond.

NORTH WYNAAD,—(Continued.)

Name by which known to Europeans.	Name by which known to Natives.	Names of Proprietors.	Names of Managers.
Emily	Terrioot	Furze and Barrington	R. W. Barrington
Fairfield	Perria Totum	G. Campbell and others	F. H. Tomlinson
Furlaugh	Do.	Ghaut Coffee Co. (Limited.)	C. B. Speechley
Farrington	....	F. H. Tomlinson	F. H. Tomlinson
Glenlee	Trichiterry	Anderson	W. Gladstone
Huntley	Huntley	J. Gordon	T. R. Richmond
Jessie	Croocherpardy	Dr. Cream	Buxy
Kelliout	Do.	C. Puddicombe	C. Puddicombe
Kenilworth	Macfarlan Totum	J. Macfarlane	W. F. Macfarlane
Kanatu Mulla	Kunatu Mulla	Tucker	J. D. Bell
Karkerry	Kukkerry	P. H. Gordon	P. H. Gordon
Langcliff	Hundy Cull	H. Dawson	W. C. Dawson
Manantoddy	Manantawaddy	Dunbar & Fraser	T. R. Richmond
Minne Ha Ha	Croocherpardy	J. Macfarlane	W. F. Macfarlane
Mary Estate	....	Carnatic Coffee Company	H. Lemesurier
Mary	Terriout	Manderson & Co.	B. Miller
Middleton	Dawson Doray Totum	Heycock Davidson	W. C. Dawson
Moodra Mulla	Moodra Mulla	Bombay & Coast Company	R. Haden and E. Quarme
Nemonie	Nemonile	J. Nicholson	J. B. Kibble
Olliout	Olliout	Forman	J. R. Malcolm
Oolygood	Oolygood	Cama & Co.	G. F. Brown
Pattery	Atty Mallay	J. Gordon	W. Gladstone
Pillay Cardoo	Pillie Kahdoo	Madras Coffee Co.	W. T. Rayne
Pandoorang	Pandurang	Cama & Co.	F. E. Richmond
Pagoda	Daivissa	P. H. Gordon	J. W. Smith
Ramsay	Thulapoora	Pandoorang and Richmond	T. R. Richmond
Richlieu	....	Rich and Richmond	F. E. Richmond

xvii

NORTH WYNAAD,—(Continued.)

Name by which known to Europeans.	Name by which known to Natives.	Names of Proprietors.	Names of Managers.
Richville	Coodray Cotta	Rich	F. E. Richmond
Ragonath	....	Cama & Co.	G. F. Brown
Reading	Bombay Totum	Sigg	H. Sigg
Rasselas	Kirrinelly	F. E. Richmond	F. E. Richmond
Soosauker	Aliam Mulla	Pandoorang	T. R. Richmond
Tata Mulla	Tatamullah	Boyd & Co.	R. Haden
Tandiote	Tandiote	Nicholas	Miller
The Hermitage	....	P. H. Gordon	J. Lowrie
Teddington	Croocherpardy	Bombay & Coast Company	R. Haden
Vellera Mulla	Vellera Mullay	Col. J. W. Wooldridge	Col. J. W. Wooldridge
Winterthur	....	Sigg Brothers	H. Sigg
Weycoon	Waycoon	Forbes & Co.	J. M. Closson
Wynaad	Wynaad	Col. Smyth	A. R. Higinbothom

SOUTH WYNAAD.

Arrahmulla	Arrahmulla	Natives	A Native
Adelaide	....	W. D. Cartwright	J. Boosey, and A. Lamond
Askeen	Perendatty	J. Smith	Owner & S. Prager
Anderose	....	H. B. Winterbotham	Owner
Annaparah	....	F. J. Ferguson & others	Native
Annettee	Pooda Culloor	Leckie & Co.	J. Fargie
Armacullah	....	J. H. Rossall	Owner
Ballia Parah	....	W. M. McCulloch	Smith
Carpen Culli	....	A. R. Hinde	Owner and Wapshaw
Charlotte	....	Leckie & Co.	C. S. Moon

SOUTH WYNAAD,—(Continued.)

Name by which known to Europeans.	Name by which known to Natives.	Names of Proprietors.	Names of Managers.
Culloor	....	Leckie & Co.	A. Wildes and E. Mitchell
Chumbatie	....	P. S. Punnett	Owner
Coombatoor	....	J. Hester, M. D.	Owner
Coonumbatta	....	R. Wardrop	
Chumbrani	....	Southern India Coffee Co.	J. Boydell
Caroline	....		L. S. Clark
Culputty	....		G. Harcourt
Charity	....	M. Rimington	Percy Guard
Catherine	Perendatty	H. B. Winterbotham	Owner
Ellumbellary Peak	Jannyoot	A. R. Hinde	Owner and Wapshaw
Emily	....	A. Lopez	Owner
Faith	Chumbra Mulla	M. Rimington	J. H. Gordon
Field, The	....	H. D. Cartwright	G. B. Elliot and Boosey
Hope	Chumbra Mulla	M. Rimington and others	W. Kennedy and H. Gordon
Kotamundah	....	G. L. Yonge and others	H. Winterbotham
Lackadie	Rendan Tote	A. Rimington	J. B. Buckham
Lancaster	Kroocher Mulla	G. J. Glasson and others	Langshawe
Maipardie	....	J. Boosey & others	Kinney
Molina	Kroocher Mulla	J. Gordon	Reid
Manara Mulla	....	A. Barnes and R. Petman	A. C. Barnes
Moota Mulla	....	Southern of India Coffee Company	Viscardi
Mowbray	....	J. G. Glasson	A. F. Schlunk
Madutella	Poodoo Rendan Tote	J. B. Buckham	Owner
Munda Mulla	....	W. Kennedy	Owner
Pootha Cooly	....	C. Wildes	Native
Palla Coon	Croocher Mulla	G. L. Yonge	Owner

SOUTH WYNAAD,—(Continued.)

Name by which known to Europeans.	Name by which known to Natives.	Names of Proprietors.	Names of Managers.
Perim Chole	Perendatty	J. Gordon	Reid
Panora Peak	Cherria Chumbra	J. H. Rossall	Owner and Gaitskell
Pootha Para	....	Southern of India Coffee Company.	C. Wildes
Prendamotele	....	G. J. Glasson	J. Jones (Lessee)
Perendatye	....	Boyd & Co.	Turner & Archer
Pokoote	....	Robson & Brown	H. H. Brown
Rimington No. 1	} Chumbra Mulla	M. Rimington	{ T. J. Ferguson
Do. No. 2			C. Kilgour
Steppanie	....	S. India Coffee Co.	Thompson and Richardson
St. Mary	....	Carter	Owner
Tanoortha	Tannyoot	S. India Coffee Co.	Jordan
Thalapaya	....	F. Jones	Owner
Vythery	....	G. J. Glasson	T. Jones
Wallace	....	H. D. Cartwright	G. B. Elliott and Boosey
Walthamstowe	....	G. J. Glasson and others	A. F. Schlunk
Virginia	....	A. Lopez	Owner

SOUTH-EAST WYNAAD.

Principally derived from Gantz' People's Almanac for 1865.

Name of Estate.	Proprietors.	Managers.
Ambillee Mulla	W. H. Sinclair	Owner
Adelphi	J. W. Minchin	P. Cherry
Balmades	Rhode	Swan
Beta Mund	Vigars	Owner
Burnstein	Lazaron and Malcolm	J. Lazaron
Balcarras	Steedman	Owner

SOUTH-EAST WYNAAD,—(*Continued.*)

Name of Estate.	Proprietors.	Managers.
Cherrumbady	Lovell and Maylor	Rodrigues
Caroline	A. Wright	Owner
Coomallay	F. Hughes	Owner
Chembillee Mullay	J. D'Silva	Owner
Ellen	Maylor	Cranley
Grange	Watts	Wright
Glenrock	J. Perrie	W. Ryan
Glendowe	Lascelles	Capps
Glendale	Do.	E. Laseron
Glen Vans	Vans Agnew	T. Murray
Guynd	J. Ouchterlony	C. Y. Reed
Goodaloor Mullay	Do.	Dickens
Hamslade	J. W. Minchin	Owner and Hawkins
Helen	Do.	J. Tyndall
Hope	Do.	Do.
Hatcham	Broomhall	Owner
Harewood	J. T. Mackenzie	Brunton
Hope	Malabar East India Co.	Fernandez
Kintail	Mackenzie and Linton	W. H. Linton
Kulliad	A. Lascelles	J. R. Malcolm
Lauriston	J. Ouchterlony	C. Y. Reed
Moyar Valley	Scott and Taylor	J. Hicks
Maramootoo	J. B. Burnett	Owner
Maryland	Lascelles	J. Brown
Mary Ann	Wright	A Native
Naiken Chola	Cox and Minchin	Native
Neddakannay	Nelamboor Rajah	Native
Nelliallum	W. Ryan	Owner
Do. Peak	J. Hollis	Owner
Needle Rock	Aboo Sait & Co.	W. Bunyan
Nundutty	J. Higginbotham	Owner
Oakley	Rhode, (Junior)	Swan
Pundaloor	Ryan	Owner
Perseverance	Malabar E. I. Co. (Ld.)	Fernandez
Provident	Malabar E. I. Co. (Ld)	Reinman
Pillee Mullah	T. Browning	Owner
Pawady Poyah	C. Godfrey	Owner
Peria Chola	J. C. Andrew	Owner
Richmond	A. Wright	Owner

SOUTH-EAST WYNAAD,—(Continued.)

Name of Estate.	Proprietors.	Managers.
Sheerdale	Miller and Lowe	A. Lowe
Strathern	A. Lascelles	—
Surry	Bates Brothers	J. Turner
Seaforth	Arbuthnot and Co.	A. Griffin
Sandy Hills	J. Ouchterlony	J. Tyndall
Suffolk	Do.	H. Coates
Wentworth	Schmidt and others	Native
Yellammulla	C. Godfrey	Owner

LIST OF COFFEE PLANTERS IN COORG, TAKEN FROM GANTZ' MADRAS PEOPLE'S ALMANAC, FOR 1865.

			No. of Acres.
Coorg Coffee Company "Limited"	Mercara Talook	Horamulnaad	7,882
Donald Stewart, Esq.	do	do	4,100
Henry Mann, Esq.	do	do	2,334
A. C. Campbell, Esq. and others	do	do	1,730
Joseph P. Hunt, Esq.	do	do	1,700
Peter James, Esq.	do	Kuggodulnaad	1,500
Alexander Bain, Esq.	do	do	1,160
Carnatic Coffee Company "Limited"	do	Horamulnaad	1,000
H. A. Mangles, Esq.	do	Halarynaad	920
Major G. M. Martin	do	Horamulnaad	828
Rev. A. Fennell, Bulthymullay Estate	do	Halarynaad	519
Bittienda Caryuppa	do	Horamulnaad	500
Messrs. Charles Grant, Lewis Ross, George Ross and W. G. Aspinall	do	Kuggodulnaad	500
William Urquhart Arbuthnot, Esq.	do	Horoornoorakulnaad	491
Kodandra Appachoo	do	Horamulnaad	423

xxii

LIST OF PLANTERS IN COORG, &c.—(*Continued.*)

			No. of Acres.
C. W. James, Esq. and R. H. James, Esq., Helenhully Estate	Mercara Talook	Horamulnaad	419
D. McPherson, Esq., M.D.	do	do	333
Matandra Appachoo	do	do	316
Cheppudi Subbiah, Esq.	do	do	304
Kongandra Appiya	do	do	200
P. V. Ragavachary and others	do	do	154
Woodiendra Daviya	do	Kuggodulnaad	101
P. Ramiengar	do	Horamulnaad	100
Mahomed Hoossain	do	do	60
S. Thimmappiya	do	do	57
P. A. Moultree, Esq.	do	Horoornoorakulnaad	50
Captain J. G. Marshall	do	do	46
Mr. C. Kamsika	do	do	45
Calavandra Caryappa and others	Paddynacknaad Talook	Kadiethnaad	50
William Burnett, Esq. and others	do	Koingherrynaad	300
Manawatty Bopoo	do	Paddynacknaad	200
Koottettira Jyappa	do	Koingherrynaad	200
Apparandra Caryappa	do	do	80
Thomas Taylor, Esq.	do	do	60
Dr. W. G. Maxwell and J. McKenzie, Esq.	Yeddaynacknaad Talook	Yeddaynacknaad	2,461
David Rose, Esq.	do	do	1,300
Reverend C. G. Richter	do	Unmuthnaad	900
Carnatic Coffee Company	do	do	600
John McKenzie, Esq.	do	do	500
Reverend H. A. Kaundinya	do	do	500
Henry P. Minchin, Esq.	do	Yeddaynacknaad	500
Messrs. Farrier and Brown	do	Unmuthnaad	500
S. G. Tipping, Esq.	do	do	360
George Anderson, Esq.	do	do	300
James Stewart, Esq.	do	Yeddaynaad	300
Colavandra Caryappa	do	do	201
William Brown, Esq.	do	do	120
Augustus Plumbe, Esq.	do	Ummuthnaad	56

LIST OF PLANTERS IN COORG, &c.—(*Continued.*)

			No. of Acres.
J. Gillibrand, Esq.	Yeddaynacknaad Talook	Yeddaynacknaad..	56
Messrs. J. Peebles & Rose	KiggutnaadTalook	Bettiethnaad	1,600
W. C. Dawson, Esq.	do	Thavulgherry-moornaad	1,000
Dr. Nicol Martin, and Sam Martin McGregor, Esq.	do	Bettiethnaad	700
W. V. Drummond, Esq.	do	Murraynaad	700
Captain Ralph N. Taylor	do	Aujigerynaad	700
Colonel W. J. Wooldridge	do	Thavulgherry-moornaad	530
Major J. Renton	do	Murraynaad	300
J. W. Savage, Esq.	do	Bettiethnaad	300
Frank Brown, Esq.	do	do	250
Messrs. Green and Denton	Nanjarajputten Talook	Soorlabee Moothnaad	750
Lieut.-Col. Cunningham & Major Grey	do	do	500
C. F. Nepean, Esq.	do	Yedayanaad	500
Mrs. E. Wright, Loúdon Valley Estate	do	SoolabeMoothnaad	350
Joseph Lacey, Esq., Lieut. J. Markham, and W. Jennings, Esq., Coomboocaud Estate	do	do	271
R. Carr, Esq., Curton Estate	do	do	200
Native holdings from one Acre and upwards in	Mercara Talook		5,592
Do do do	Paddynacknaad Talook		3,341
Do do do	Yeddaynacknaad Talook		3,604
Do do do	KiggutnaadTalook		1,918
Do do do	Nanjarajputten Talook		652
Do do do	Yeloosaverasee-may Talook		198
			61,516

COONOOR.

Name of Estate.	Extent.	Proprietors.	Managers.
Adderley	400 Acres.	Messrs. Arbuthnot and Co.	Clarkson and Thomas
Ben Hope	66 do	J. G. Herklots	Owner
Brodsworth	100 do	C. Sanderson	Owner
Coonoor Ghât	50 do	Mahanjee Sait	Owner
Charles' Hope	70 do	Reilly and Woodfall	Reily
Chelmsford	250 do	T. Staines	Owner
Chengal	250 do	Mullaly, (Junior)	Owner
Colacumbe	200 do	T. Stanes	Owner
Carolina	80 do	Major Sweet	Owner
Craigmore	80 do	Major Hodgson	Stainbank (Lessee)
....	50 do	Captain Fuller	Owner
Droog	200 do	W. Mullaly, (Senior)	Owner
Glenmore	170 do	Hunter and Allan	A. Allan
Hilgrove	250 do	Colonel Woodfall and Marden	Darling, Frank & Reily, (Lessees)
Hulicul	150 do	Stainbank and Chambers	Owners
Krillarama	50 do	Nanjaparow	Owner
Kartari	120 do	Messrs. Vincent and de Facien	Owners
Louisiana	100 do	Major Sweet	Owner
Little Ireland	150 do	C. Murray	Owner
Neriolay	300 do	J. G. Herklots	Owner
Pilloor	400 do	J. Hunter	Owner
Reading	180 do	C. Sanderson	Owner
Runnymede	300 do	T. Stanes	Owner
Vellanec (Tea Estate)	100 do	Carnatic Coffee Co.	J. Gordon
Woodlands	150 do	Stainbank	J. McIvor
Seddipulli, No. 1	200 do	Mr. J. Hayne	} Owner
Do. No. 2.	200 do	Do.	
Do. No. 3.	100 do	R. Grove	Owner
Do. No. 4.	80 do	W. Mullaly, (Senior)	Owner

ERRATA.

Page 18 for "knowledge of superstition," read "knowledge of *this* superstition."
,, 22 ,, "magnitude for the crops," read "magnitude *of* the crops."
,, 63 ,, "object being to exclusive eternal influences," read "object being to *exclude* external influences."
,, 73 ,, "filled over them," read "*felled* over them."
,, 114 ,, "unto the mould," read "*into* the mould."
,, 129 ,, "waste of sap, vitality, and lime," read "waste of sap, vitality, and *time.*"
,, 141 ,, "Islands of China," read "Islands of *Chinca.*"
,, 157 ,, "they will then come whiter," read "they will then *become* whiter."
,, 167 ,, "at just in use," read "at *first* in use."
,, 175 ,, "selling Rs. 30 to 40 per acre," read "selling *at* Rs. 30 to 40."
,, 181 ,, "exceeding double quantity," read "exceeding double *that* quantity."
,, 202 ,, "contusion of thought," read "*confusion* of thought."
,, 206 ,, "and cut bloody," read "and cut *boldly.*"
,, 207 ,, "as lightly as possible," read "as *tightly* as possible."

CHAPTER I.

COFFEE BOTANICALLY AND PHYSIOLOGICALLY CONSIDERED.

COFFEE (Coffea Arabica) belongs to the natural family *Rubiaceæ*, and to the class *Pentandria Monogynia* of Linnæus. In the Arabic language *Kahwah* is the name for the liquor of Coffee, in the Turkish *Capee*, hence the common name *Coffee*.

THE Coffee tree, or more properly shrub, is of a graceful and elegant form, and when permitted to grow naturally attains a height, under favorable circumstances, of from fifteen to twenty feet, slender and at the upper part dividing into long drooping branches, which seldom grow to any great thickness.

The leaves are evergreen, opposite, very shiny on the upper surface, elliptical, pointed, and between three and four inches long; they are connected with the branches by short foot stalks, and somewhat resemble those of the Portuguese laurel: each pair is usually two to four inches apart from the next on the branch.

The flowers are white and small, and very like those of the Jessamine, both in scent and appearance; they are botanically described to be axillary, sessile, calyx monopetalous, funnel-shaped, cut at the limb into fine reflexed lanceolate segments. They grow in groups varying from four to sixteen in number, in each group, from the axils of the leaves.

The bark is almost smooth, of a greyish brown.

The fruit or berries which succeed the blossom, are at first dark-green, then changing as they approach maturity to light yellow, and light red, until they become of a dark crimson, like a ripe cherry, which tint announces that they are ready for gathering.

The pulp of this berry has a sweetish insipid taste and is slightly glutinous; within it are enclosed two hard, oval seeds, one side of which is convex, and the other flat, and having a straight furrow inscribed through the latter side lengthwise; while within the berry the flat sides of the seed face each other. These seeds are generally termed "beans," not from their resemblance to that pulse, but, as Chambers's Encyclopædia informs us, from the Arabic word "bunn;" they are enclosed in a cartilaginous membrane, which, from its faint strawey colour and peculiar consistency, has received the name of "Parchment."

Besides the C. Arabica, there are other kinds, of which the C. Mauritiana, when prepared in the same manner as the C. Arabica, has a bitter unpleasant taste and the property of being slightly emetic.

Some Botanists have named only two distinct species of the Coffee tree, the *C. Arabica* and the *C. Occidentalis;* others again, are of opinion that the different sorts are only varieties, resulting from soil, climate, and modes of culture.

The tree is a native of Arabia Felix and Ethiopia, and was first introduced to the notice of Europeans by Rauwolfius, in 1573; but Alpinus in 1591 was the first who scientifically described it.

The Dutch were the first to introduce the plant into Europe. Having procured some berries at Mocha, which were carried to Batavia, and there planted, a specimen was sent to Amsterdam, in the year 1690, by Governor Wilson, where it bore fruit and produced many young trees; from these the East Indies and most of the gardens of Europe were furnished.

It was first cultivated in Britain by Bishop Compton in 1696. In 1714 a plant was presented by the Magistrates of Amsterdam, to the French King, Louis XIV.; this plant was placed at Marley under the care of the Jussieu, and from this source plants were forwarded some years afterwards, to the French islands in the West Indies, from whence all the Coffee plants now found there, derive their origin.*

"The Coffea Arabica, from its being the principal producer of Coffee, is the chief and most useful, but besides this, other species are cultivated in other parts of the world, on account of their commercial value, all of which though now regarded as separate species, owe their origin to the Coffea Arabica, which was first introduced into Arabia about the commencement of the 15th century, from Enarea and *Caffa* in Southern Abyssinia, to which countries it is indigenous."†

Coffee contains many valuable medicinal properties, principally as an anti-soporific, and a remedy in cases of

---

* Rhind's History of the Vegetable Kingdom.
† Beverages we infuse,—*Blackwood's Magazine.*

narcotic poisoning. From the stimulating and enlivening effect the beverage is found to exercise on the system, one cannot but suppose that it contains a considerable amount of nutrition, though we see in one writer,* both tea and coffee put down as articles which contain no real nutriment. On the other hand, a periodical† informs us that there is much nutriment contained in the Oil of Coffee, or Caffeine, which we may see floating on the surface of the pure beverage.

That medical men have frequently found Coffee the best form of administering nourishment and stimulant, to persons rescued from starvation, by cold or hunger, is a strong argument in its favor, especially as ardent spirits administered under the same circumstances will often prove fatal.

Coffee is also valuable as a disinfecting agent. "It is useful to purify any place having an offensive smell or foul air. The Coffee beans should be roasted in the vicinity of the room to be purified, and when they have attained their brown colour, and while quite hot, removed to the room and placed in the centre, in the same pan or chatty in which they were torrified. The doors and windows should be closed, and in half an hour, by which time the Coffee will have become cool, the room will be rendered thoroughly purified and the air sweet."‡

Which of us does not know the grateful fragrance of a cup of good Coffee, whether on the midnight railway journey in the melting heat of India, or before a skating expedition on a frosty morning in England?

---

* Galton's Art of Travel.
† *Household Words*, 1851.
‡ Dr. Shortt.

Doctor Shortt also enumerates some diseases, in which Coffee has been found efficacious.

"Grindell used it in cases of intermittent fever. It is sometimes very useful in relieving headache. * * * As a stomachic in some forms of dyspepsia; as an astringent in diarrhœa, and a stimulant to the cerebro-spinal system, in some nervous disorders;" in curing gout, asthma, &c.

It will be apparent that the merits of Coffee as a beverage, would have remained quite unknown, but for the discovery of the means of using it roasted. For this discovery we are indebted to the Persians, who practised this method of preparing it long before it was known in Arabia. The name of the fire-worshipper who first initiated the idea, is unknown.

We are informed,* that in the middle of the 15th century, the Mufti of Aden, when on a journey to pay homage to his superior, saw the processes of roasting, grinding, and boiling the Coffee, and that he on his return, introduced the discovery into Arabia. There was considerable opposition made by the "true believers," at first, to its use, who judging from its stimulating powers that it must have an intoxicating effect, considered it to be under the ban of the Prophet.

The Sultan, however, issued a proclamation, declaring its use lawful and proper, upon which numerous booths for its sale, were at once erected.

The consumption of Coffee is exceedingly great in Turkey,

---

* *Household Words.*

and this fact may be in a great measure accounted for, by the strict prohibition which the Moslem religion lays against the use of wine and spirituous liquors.

So necessary was Coffee at one time considered amongst the people, that the refusal to supply it in reasonable quantity to a wife, was reckoned among the legal causes for a divorce.

The Turks drink their Coffee very hot and strong, and without Sugar, occasionally they put in, when boiling, a clove or two bruised, or a few seeds of starry aniseed, or some of the lesser cardamoms, or a drop of essence of amber.

In England, the use of Coffee met at first with violent opposition, as has indeed been the case with almost every new article introduced among our conservative countrymen; it was denounced as a "Hell-drink," or "Hell-poison," or by some other equally unflattering title, and a heavy tax was imposed on it by the legislature of so much a gallon.

This method of taxation is singular, as, of course, it might be a very mawkish drink or otherwise, at the option of the seller.

It was brought to England first by a Turkey merchant returning from a voyage to the Levant, in the time of Cromwell; he was accompanied by a Greek named Pasqua, who understood the art of preparing the beverage. This man founded a Coffee-house in London, which prospered so exceedingly, that it is said, in twelve months there were as many Coffee-houses in London as in Constantinople.

This merchant was Daniell Edwards, who is well worthy of being remembered with gratitude by lovers of Coffee, a drink which, far more than tea, cheers without inebriating.

Coffee-houses from that period formed an important feature in the economy of the Metropolis, and the very name of "Coffee-house" is replete with associations of the literature of the last century.

It is not, however, only the berry of the Coffee plant which is a febrifuge; I am informed that an infusion made from its leaves have, in the absence of more powerful tonics, been found very beneficial. This is not much to be wondered at, when we recollect that this plant is one of the *Cinchonaceæ*.

It seems to be one of the most inviolable rules of Nature, guided as she is by a bountiful Providence, to permit no evil to exist, without having provided at hand a remedy; and doubtless the further we advance in the knowledge of nature and her doings, the more unexceptional this arrangement will be found: under this supposition, it is asserted that Coffee grows best in feverish localities, which I consider, from my own experience, to be extremely probable.

A decoction made from the leaves, dried in a peculiar manner, forms, I believe, an agreeable beverage, but the difficulty in procuring this preparation in perfection appears to consist, in discovering the proper method of drying the leaves, so as to preserve a greenish tint, and this is a secret which is not known to Europeans, though Doctor Gardner exhibited specimens of the leaves, dried for use as tea, in the Great Exhibition, and took out a patent to protect his method.

Coffee-tea is the common beverage of the inhabitants of Sumatra, and cannot therefore, be considered as otherwise than wholesome and nourishing; though, unfortunately, from the experiments which have been made, it does not appear to possess the deliciously aromatic flavour of the Coffee bean or of tea leaves, but to resemble more a mixture of both.

In answer to this objection, however, it must be borne in mind that the taste for many valuable exotic productions is only acquired by habit.

When required for use, the Coffee leaves should be dried fresh on a pan, over a slow fire, until they have become of a clear brown colour; by which process the Theine or Caffeine or Volatile oil becomes fixed, and they can then be infused, in the same manner as tea leaves in a tea pot.

Though possessing slightly tonic and stimulant properties, it has not nearly the same exciting effect as an infusion of the roasted bean; however, as it could be produced and sold at one-fifth or one-quarter of the cost of the latter, it might be a valuable acquisition to many, who, from the high price of the bean, are precluded from purchasing it. It may be sweetened with sugar and diluted with milk in the same manner as tea, and will then be an innocent, pleasant, and nutritious drink.

* "Thus, while the public are supplied with a good and useful drink, the planter will have an additional source of revenue."

The price of prepared Coffee leaves in Sumatra is about one anna per lb., and this price is remunerative to the planter. It could thus be imported and sold in England at 2d. per lb.

Dried Coffee leaves contain about $1\frac{1}{4}$ per cent. of Theine,

---

* Dr. Shortt.

or ¼ per cent. more than the bean; they also contain more of another characteristic principle of Coffee, Caffeic Acid, the only difference in the properties of either being apparently, that while the bean contains about 12 per cent. of fat and 7 per cent. of sugar, the leaf possesses but little of either.

We cannot dismiss the physiological consideration of Coffee better than by introducing the following extract from Ferguson's Ceylon Common-Place Book for the year 1860, entitled, "Analysis of Coffee":—

"The paper we publish below, cannot but be of interest and value to our Planting readers:

Lime, if it could be procured cheaply and in quantity, is, of course, one of the best applications to Coffee Estates, for it forms 60 per cent. of the ashes of the plant. Doctor Gygax, who analyzed the wood as well as the berries, was of opinion that one cwt. per acre of lime would generally suffice. The difficulty is to get the lime; for, although excellent Dolomite abounds in many parts of the Coffee districts, the expense of burning, carrying, and applying has been hitherto found to be too high in most cases. It becomes quite a different matter where Planters are told that the Quartz and Gneiss, which are found on every Coffee Estate, are when pounded, valuable as constituents of manure. This accords with experience, for the finest Coffee grows amongst masses of Gneiss, gradually decomposing from the influence of the climate on its felspathic constituents.

About 10 years ago Mr. Herepath analyzed 150 grains of fine West Indian Coffee berries, for the purpose of determining the best manure for the West Indian Coffee Estates. The results did not differ materially from those now arrived at. Deducting the Carbonic Acid, 100 grains of ash gave as their principal constituents,

Phosphate of Lime	45·551
Phosphoric Acid	12·801
Potash	16·512
Soda	6·787
Magnesia	5·942
Lime	2·329
Sulphate of Lime	1·751

with small quantities of Sulphuric Acid, Chloride of Sodium, and Silicic Acid.

"Consequently," remarked Mr. Herepath, "for every ton of dried Coffee beans that is raised on a plantation, the Proprietor must consider about the following quantities of the various mineral substances, as having been removed from his land:—

	lbs.	oz.
Phosphoric Acid	27	14½
Sulphuric Acid	0	13½
Potash	11	4
Soda	4	10
Chloride of Sodium or Common Salt	0	7
Lime	18	14
Magnesia	4	1
Silicic Acid or Silica	0	5
	68	5

When bone-dust, cow-dung, and wood-ashes can be obtained and applied cheaply, of course nothing can be better; a little pounded Gneiss might be an improvement. Failing bone-dust and cow-dung, then recourse must be had to ammoniacal manures, (such as Guano) and to Lime. The Dolomite of the interior contains, according to Doctor Gygax, the proper proportion of Phosphoric Acid in the shape of Apatite or Phosphate of Lime.

PLANTERS' ASSOCIATION.

Extract of Proceedings of a Committee Meeting held on Saturday, the 20th November 1858.

Read letter from Mr. Walters, offering a chemical analysis of Ceylon plantation Coffee by Mr. Herepath, Analytical Chemist, Bristol, on our paying £5 fee, paid by him for Lime, and publish results of experiments when ascertained.

Resolved,—That the offer be accepted.

Extract from Proceedings of a Committee Meeting held on Monday, the 27th December 1858.

Read Walters' letter from Herepath, Analytical Chemist, on chemical analysis of Coffee.

Resolved,—That the letter be published.

(True extracts.)

ALEX. BROWN,
Secretary.

(COPY.)

BRISTOL, ENGLAND, *June* 13th, 1858.

W. H. WALTERS, ESQ.,
Bambra Ella Estate, Ceylon.

SIR,—I have studied the subject of your letter through

the Rev. Walter Marriott, and having made the necessary experiments and calculations, I have to report that 1,000 lbs. of raw Coffee berries of Ceylon plantation growth contain as under, of mineral ingredients :—

	lbs.
Potash	37
Lime	2¾
Magnesia	5¾
Peroxyde of Iron	¼
Sulphuric Acid	2½
Chlorine	¾
Carbonic Acid	11¾
Phosphoric Acid	7
	67¾

I do not know the exact analysis of your granitic rocks, but presume they must contain a little potash, lime and iron, and possibly magnesia; but the ash is too alkaline for me to think that all the potash comes from that source; the principal portion of it must come from the felled wood; the carbonic acid, of course, comes from the atmosphere, but the principal ingredients you require as manure I conceive to be phosphoric acid, sulphate of lime, and carbonate of magnesia. About 100 lbs. of Peruvian guano, with 7 or 8 lbs. of ground gypsum, 10 lbs. of magnesian limestone, and 11 lbs. of salt, mixed up with your vegetable or the ashes of the wood clearance, and some of your granite or quartz, pounded, would, I think, make a good manure for 1,000 lbs. of raw berries. I cannot calculate what would be necessary to supply the woody matter of the trees with nourishment, as

I do not know their chemical analysis, but should imagine that if the whole of the woody matter or their ashes were returned to the land, it would be sufficient; but if any part of the vegetation is not economised, of course that loss must be made up in manure.

I am, Sir,

Your's respectfully,

(Signed)   W. HEREPATH, F.C.S.,

Professor of Chemistry.

(5 Guineas.)

CHAPTER II.

SOME ACCOUNT OF CEYLON, WYNAAD, COORG, THE NEILGHERRIES, MYSORE, AND THE SHEVAROYS, AS COFFEE-PRODUCING DISTRICTS.

COFFEE is grown in Arabia, Africa, S. India, Ceylon, Java, the West Indian Islands, the Brazils, Peru, and in the Mauritius, in mountainous regions where the climate is mild and temperate; but as my experience as a planter has been entirely gathered in Ceylon and India, this work will doubtless be found more applicable to its cultivation in these localities, than in any of the other countries above-mentioned.

By whom, or at what period, the Coffee tree was first introduced into Ceylon and India, is not, I believe, known, but that this occurred at least two centuries ago, there is little doubt.

It is probable, that it may have found its way along the Coast, from Southern Arabia in Mussulman craft at a very early period: indeed, the natives of Mysore have a tradition that Coffee was introduced in Munzerabad or Chick-Moogloor, by an Arab 400 or 500 years ago, as will be seen hereafter.

It is stated that trees then of a great age were found in

the Coorg territory more than 40 years ago; and in Manantoddy, Wynaad, a tree, supposed to be 30 years old, if not more, was discovered by a Captain Bevan, the Commandant of the small garrison of the place, twenty-six years ago, who thought the circumstance of sufficient consequence to be reported to Government. However, the systematic cultivation of Coffee, on the Indian Peninsula by Europeans, does not appear to date more than about thirty years back: but in an old book published in 1802, I have seen it stated that Coffee had then been some time cultivated in *Arabia, America,* and the *East* and West Indies.*

Dr. Shortt states, "It was introduced into Ceylon by the Arabs, prior to the invasion of that island by the Portuguese. The Dutch introduced the Coffee plant into Batavia in 1690, and at the same time commenced its cultivation in Ceylon. On the cession of this territory by the Dutch, its culture was continued by the Cingalese, and during the British occupation of Ceylon the Mahomedan inhabitants bartered its produce at Galle and Colombo."

In Ceylon, it appears to have been originally cultivated by the natives, with a very different object to that which now forms our incentive, namely, in order that its sweetly-scented blossom might be used for decorating the Buddhist shrines; and accordingly the plant was first discovered at Hangurankette, where there were at one time a king's palace, and a large Buddhist's establishment. From this nucleus, it had sown itself over a large tract of forest; when the value of the produce of the plant had become known to the natives, and the Kandian kingdom had passed into the

---

* Reference is here evidently made to the operations of the Dutch of Batavia.

hands of the English, a wealthy and intelligent native bought the entire mountain on which the Coffee was growing, from Government, at the then upset price of 5s. an acre. This gentleman has realized, as may be supposed, a handsome fortune from his purchase.

A gentleman residing on the Neilgherries, informed me recently, that there is a wild description of coffee to be found growing in the forests on those mountains, and that it is well known to the Todars or aboriginal inhabitants. I have some doubts, however, as to the correctness of this statement, the probable solution of which, is that seeds carried from plantations by birds, squirrels, or other creatures, may have fallen and germinated in those spots where the supposed wild Coffee is found.

Sir Edward Barnes, that energetic Governor to whom belongs the credit of uniting Kandy and the Western Coast of Ceylon at Colombo, by one of the finest roads in the world, was the first European who brought English energy and capital to bear upon the pursuit now under discussion, in Ceylon.

His estate, which was first planted in about 1825, is still under cultivation, and is now managed by his son. It is named Gangaroowa, and is situated about four miles from Kandy, on the banks of the river Mahavilla Ganga, facing the Botanical Gardens called Peradenia, a visit to which latter, forms one of the pleasantest drives in the vicinity of the Mountain Capital.

Besides this, there are some other very old estates in existence, Condesalle, 6 miles from Kandy, having been originally planted about forty years ago, and others near the town of Gampola about the same time.

These facts are encouraging to the intending speculator, as they tend to shew how durable is the value of property of this sort; and, indeed, I have no doubt whatever, but that a Coffee Estate might, with careful cultivation, be kept up for any number of years.

Mountainous regions alone in India and Ceylon are chosen for this cultivation, and the Kandian Province, forming the mountain zone, and in extent about one-fourth of the island, is now the theatre of operations so extensively carried on, as to have earned for Ceylon the position of a Colony so flourishing, as to surpass all other parts of Her Majesty's dominions, in the quantity and quality of its Coffee.

The Western Ghauts of Southern India, and their branches stretching into Coorg and Mysore, and the Neilgherries, now show many a smiling plantation on their slopes, which, spreading industry and comfort into many a previously impoverished village, render the Coffee planter a benefactor of his species, well worthy the protection and encouragement of the Government, which his energy tends to enrich.

It is my intention to give in this chapter a short description of each of the districts abovenamed, and I will commence with Ceylon, it being of the most importance.

The town of Kandy, little more than half a century ago the stronghold of a savage tyrant, now the centre of industry and civilization to a district which exports annually produce to the value of nearly one million and a half sterling, is 72 miles from Colombo, with which it communicates daily by two mail coaches. It is situated within a valley, and with its lake, churches, and villas nestling in the surrounding verdure, forms an almost romantic picture of beauty. In this town there are many European and native shops of high order, which drive a brisk trade; two manufactories of machinery which almost render the planter independent of Sheffield or Birmingham; two Banks of sterling reputation, and hotels which, though much abused, can accommodate a large number of visitors. The Barracks, which usually contain from 600 to 800 troops, and numerous visitors to the place besides those who are resident, give a dignified and stirring appearance to this little city. I must not omit to mention "the Pavilion," or summer residence of the Governor, which is surrounded by tastefully laid out gardens. This Palace forms the scene of an annual gay entertainment, to which most of the lieges of the Kandian Province resort.

Kandy is connected with Colombo by a most excellent carriage road, which is, as a work of engineering skill, universally praised; this road, as I said before, was made in the government of Sir Edward Barnes, and is the more remarkable, from the satin-wood bridge at Peradenia, an arched tunnelling through a massive boulder, and the Kaduganava Pass. It is said that the old Kandian chronicles contained a prophecy, to the effect that their fastness would be lost to them, when the stranger should pass through mountain and over the river, and it was from a knowledge of superstition that Sir E. Barnes caused the road to pass through the rock in question, the bridge over the Mahavilla Ganga being, of course, a necessity.

The different districts within 30 miles of Kandy, which they communicate with by excellent macadamized cart roads, are Cornegalle, Matella, Madoolkelle, Knuckles, Rangalla, Mada-Maha-Newera, Pusilava, Rambodde, Gampola, Cotmalie, Dimboola, Ambegamoa, Hewahette, and Maturatta, besides Badulla and Happootella beyond Newera Ellia, and about 80 miles from Kandy.

The roads are kept up by Government, and about 16,000 coolies are regularly employed on them, under the superintendence of Commissioners and their subordinate Officers. Carts ply continually between Colombo and the districts mentioned above, supplying the estates with rice and other necessaries, and convey back the crops to the Coast, at the average approximate rate of 2s. or 2s. 3d. per bushel for the rice they bring up, and from 7d. to 15d. for the coffee they take down.

Rice of good quality, usually costs on the Coast about 5s. or 6s. per bushel; adding this to the rate of cart hire named, the average cost on the estates is from 7s. 6d. to 8s. 6d. per bushel; it is, therefore, usually supplied to the coolies at a fixed price of 8s., there being sometimes a profit on the Estate books, and sometimes a loss. A cooly is allowed to buy from the store one bushel per month, but other supplies, with the exception of cumblies, are not issued to the coolies on the estates.

Labour is drawn from Southern India, the Districts of Madura, Tinnevelly, Tanjore, Trichinopoly, and Madras, supplying the greater number, though Mysore furnishes a considerable contingent. The coolies are brought by Canganies, who are under advance from the Estate Managers, in order that they may make a small loan, for preliminary expenses to each cooly who enrols himself in their gangs. The usual time for their arrival in Ceylon, is between May and October, and for returning to their own country, between January and April; many coolies remain two or three years in Ceylon on the same estate, while others will only remain one season: on most estates it is usual for about a third of the coolies to leave for their country every year in rotation. The ferry by which they cross at Manaar, is conducted under Government supervision, and facilities are also afforded them, of crossing by Steamer between Colombo and Tuticoreen, Negapatam, and other ports on the South Eastern Coast, on the payment of a trifling sum.

The legislature has provided just and impartial enactments for regulating the conduct of master and servant, entitled the "*Labour Ordinance,*" by which both the coolies themselves and their employers are greatly benefitted.

The rate of pay for coolies, throughout all the planting districts, is 8*d.* per diem for men, and 6*d.* for women and children. The Canganies, or gangers, are paid in proportion to their value, either as to their ability to keep a large number of coolies in their gangs, or their influence and fidelity in working them; some Canganies get as much as £5, and others as little as 15*s.* per month.

Cingalese labor is always available for contract works, such as felling, clearing, building lines or stores, &c., and is cheap and satisfactory when thus employed; the native sawyers and carpenters are also good workmen.

The Coffee crops are all cured at Colombo which is the shipping port, and works of the greatest magnitude and perfection, are there kept up for this purpose: the general charge for the curing is 4*s.* 6*d.* per cwt.

WYNAAD.

WYNAAD is a District about 70 miles long and averaging about 25 in width, situated above the Western ghauts of Southern India in latitude 11° or 12°; it is bounded by Coorg, Mysore, the Neilgherries, and the ghauts in question, and is divided into North, South, and South-East Wynaad. Wynaad contains no town of any magnitude, though Manantoddy in the North, Culputty in the South, and Goodaloor in the South-East Division, ought perhaps to be so styled. The principal of these, Manantoddy, was formerly garrisoned by native troops under command of a European Officer, and figures in the Despatches of Colonel Wellesley, in the time of Tippoo's wars; there have been no troops here, however, for some years. The Cutcherry, Police and Post Offices, with a traveller's bungalow, are the Government buildings of the place, and there are besides one or two private bungalows, a native bazaar, Parsee's shop, and a Club House, which is the resort of the surrounding planters, when business, sickness, or the desire for a brief social intercourse, lead them to visit the place.

North Wynaad is connected with the Coast by three roads, which descend the ghauts at Terriout, Cotiaddy, and Perria; with South Wynaad by two; one by Culputty and another viâ Terriout; there is also road to Mysore, and one to Ootacamund viâ Goodaloor. South Wynaad communicates with the Coast at Calicut by the Tambracherry Ghaut.

None of these roads are opened for wheeled traffic, except in the fine weather, during which season parts may be made available where the gradient admits of it.

The coffee crops are taken to the Coast at Tellicherry and Calicut, where there are several curing establishments, by means of bullocks from the Mysore country, which are brought in annually for this purpose about crop time, in large herds, and the cheapness of transport or otherwise depends on the supply of cattle and the magnitude for the crops; the rates have averaged in the present year from 7 to 13 Annas per bushel, (10½d. to 1s. 7½d.)

Labour is fluctuating and uncertain, the supply being generally inadequate to the demand. It is drawn from Mysore principally, though many estates employ a resident gang of "locals."

The Canarese coolies generally come into Wynaad between April and July, in gangs under charge of a maistry, as in Ceylon, and leave between January and March, leaving a far smaller proportion of their number, behind them, than in the same case in Ceylon.

The coolies are quite free to come and go, the law not binding them to work for any specified time, except under special written contract; whereas in Ceylon, a day's labour, unless express stipulation is made to the contrary, is considered to constitute an agreement for a month's service.

The fact of the excessive cheapness of food in their native country, which enables them to subsist for many months, on the savings of a few weeks' wages, earned in Wynaad, added to the natural sloth, inherent in the Asiatic character, are strong inducements to the Canarese people to remain idle. They subsist principally on a grain termed Raggee, four Annas worth of which will support a man for a week.

Another cause for the shortness of time during which the

Canarese coolies remain at work on the estates, is, that they are required to gather in the grain and other crops in their own villages.

That class of labour, termed "local," consisting of Errawers, Adiyars, Cooroombers, Punyars, &c., is capricious and desultory, and although these people do the entire work on one or two small estates, they are generally the servants of paddy owners, either in this district, or in the adjacent one, Coorg. Long usage, joined to the traditional feeling of subjection, dating from the time when they were slaves in the eye of the law, as well as in fact, render them entirely subservient to their native masters and former owners, and hence it is, when paddy cultivation is in progress, few can be got to work on estates; though when the works of ploughing, sowing, and reaping, are over, and maintenance would be only an unproductive burden on the paddy field owners, they are sent to work on the adjacent Coffee estates, where they are gladly employed.

Small estates can get on tolerably well with this labor, and a few Canarese, who may generally be depended on, about the commencement of the monsoon, who will help to complete the important works of that season, and again return to their country, leaving a small portion of their number on the estate, at a season when work is slack.

The "locals" are most profitably employed on buildings and small clearings.

On estates where the principal works are extensions, however this labour has not been found by any means adequate, inasmuch as it is at the very time, that a large gang is required for pitting, that labor is not forthcoming, owing to the causes named above; many estates, therefore, have succeeded in introducing a system of contracts, issued to natives from the adjacent Coasts. These contracts are high, but when successfully carried out, are nevertheless exceedingly advantageous and remunerative.

Being fully convinced of the total insufficiency of these sources of labour for carrying on works on an extensive scale, a Company formed for the cultivation of coffee, with great trouble and expense, made the experiment of introducing into Wynaad, Tamil coolies from the same districts as those which supply the Ceylon, Mauritius, Natal, and the West Indian labour markets: but notwithstanding every effort which was made to render them comfortable and contented, it was found impossible to induce them to settle down; from the first, they evinced a dislike to the district, and finally absconded. This was only to be accounted for by the following facts; that this was to them a strange country; 2nd, the difference of season, and excessive wetness of the monsoon, which produced dysentery and other complaints; and 3rd, the comparative liability of all low country people, to be attacked by fever, on residing in these Hill districts, until acclimatized.

I am still, however, of opinion, that labour will eventually have to be procured from this or some other sources, in addition to those already tried, in order to render coffee planting in Wynaad on a large scale successful. This cannot be done by one proprietor, or even by one Company however; the *planters must combine*, and strengthen their object by their *unanimous exertions*, before this or any great and important undertaking like this, can be successfully carried out. It was said the other day, in a report on the condition of India, "the natives *combine*, the Europeans *compete*," every one knows how true that remark is; if it were not so with planters, there is no undertaking, however, at present apparently impossible, which could not be accomplished, either as regards the improvement of their own interests and prospects, or the welfare of the masses. This will apply to a community as fully as to a nation.

To the planter who would repeat the experiment referred to above, I offer a few remarks on the best steps to be taken with this view.

1st.—One of the causes to which I attribute the success of Tamil labour in Ceylon, is, that from the great difficulty the coolies find in returning to their own country, they are compelled to be more dependent on their employer, who finds it his interest to take as good care of them as possible. A march of 150 miles by the one route, and some 80 or 90 by the other, followed by a sea voyage, lies between them and their home.

Another reason, doubtless, is the extensiveness of a system by which 120,000 of their own people are, on an average, domiciled in the country to which they are going; so that it hardly resembles a new country to them at all.

There systematic arrangements for supplying them with good wholesome food, at prices which they can easily afford to pay, are made (and this they know beforehand) at a time when food is hardly obtainable at all in their own villages. All these arrangements, and former precedents communicated to them by their own relatives, who have themselves tried the experiment, point to the existence of a grand organization and system, and the Malabar coolie going to Ceylon, knows as well what he is going to, as the Irish labourer going to reap the crops of England. This system is the result of the *combination* of the Ceylon planters, who will all pay their coolies alike, all charge the same sum for rice, &c., and all meet together as members of an Association which counts its members by the hundred, to consult and determine for the general good.

2nd.—In choosing a new field for supplying Wynaad with labour, I think it ought to be at a considerable distance, in order to induce the immigrants to *depend* on their new employer, and at once to reconcile themselves to settle down contentedly, to take an interest in and render their habitations cleanly and comfortable, and to make little vegetable gardens for the production of articles of diet for themselves. Contentedness and a feeling of being settled and provided for, will tend more to render them healthy than almost anything else; and, therefore, any course of treatment which will tend in this direction should be adopted.

It appears that a gentleman who was deputed from Ceylon to visit Ganjam, to report on its capabilities as a labor producing country, made a satisfactory and promising return. Without doubt one of the greatest difficulties that will present itself is the name for feverishness which this district possesses, and that it proves very much so, during certain seasons of the year, cannot be denied; this drawback can only be met by sanitary arrangements, such as erecting the coolies' lines on dry and moderately elevated situations, *protected as much as possible from the easterly winds*, supplying good *well-water*, and enforcing cleanliness amongst the coolies themselves, and, above all, supplying abundance of good " boiled rice" as food.

From what I have universally observed, of the treatment of coolies when sick, by planters generally, I feel that it is unnecessary to recommend that proper medical treatment be found for them, under these circumstances, as humanity and kindliness has already ensured them this, in almost every case.

3rd.—In getting coolies on lengthened engagements, it would be important to ascertain what assistance the Government would give, to render such agreements actually binding, what punishment would be inflicted on deserters if apprehended, and what steps the authorities would take to apprehend such.

4th.—It will also be most important to recruit only among agriculturists, and persons accustomed to out-door labour, avoiding cotton-spinners, silk-weavers, cheroot makers, &c., residents in towns and especially Military cantonments.

5th.—The importer of foreign labour should take peculiar pains to ascertain that the agreements coolies sign had been first clearly and distinctly translated and explained to them, and to ensure this a competent and respectable person should attest the fact on the back of the contract, signing his declaration in the presence of a Magistrate, if possible. This is necessary to render a labour agreement binding in Ceylon, by the new Labor Ordinance, and will enable the planter to feel sure that the coolies have not been inveigled or induced to sign by false representations. This is the more especially to be guarded against, as the class of persons who earn a nefarious livelihood, as native cooly agents, will not usually scruple to hold out all kind of impossible promises to the coolies, and engage them on any terms, being quite indifferent, whether they remain at their destination, when once the commission is paid.

If, after arriving on the Estate, the coolies find they have been deceived, and that the style of work they are required to do is different from what they were promised, that they will receive less pay or different treatment, they will not remain, not till they distinguish between the native contractor who really deceived them and their employer, who would probably be quite ignorant as to the real causes of their dissatisfaction.

6th.—Maistries should be shrewd, respectable men, and they also should be made to understand that they will be paid in proportion to the strength of their gang, say 8 Annas per head per month, thus every desertion would cost them 8 Annas, which would make it their interest to try and keep the men steady and contented. Additional remuneration might be promised them, contingent on their general good conduct and length of service.

7th.—It is a difficult task in Wynaad, under present circumstances, to supply quantities of "*boiled* rice,"* on which it would be necessary to feed the coolies. This is not generally used by the local inhabitants, whose food is princi-

---

* Rice is described as "boiled," when it has been boiled and dried, before being separated from the husk. "Raw rice" being simply obtained from the paddy, without having undergone this operation. The latter appears to agree with natives who do not make rice their only staple of food, but with those who live exclusively on rice, it produces dysentery and other troublesome and dangerous complaints.

pally raggee, or *raw* rice. Should an importation of foreign labour on a large scale be attempted, it will be, therefore, necessary to import rice for their subsistence from Bengal as is done in Ceylon. This could be brought by ship to Tellicherry, Cannanore, or Calicut, or else to Madras, whence it can be forwarded by rail to Bangalore, and then per bandies viâ Mysore, in the dry weather, to Manantoddy. A great want like this, however, would doubtless be met by those enterprising European gentlemen who have already established a considerable trade on this Coast.

THE NEILGHERRY HILLS.

THE highest of these mountains, forms the culminating point of this part of India, and runs up to upwards of 8,000 feet above the sea. At this great elevation is situated the town of Ootacamund, the sanitarium of the Madras Presidency, containing several handsome private residences, a Club, Hotel, and several European and native shops.

This place is the annual resort of most of the beauty and fashion of Madras and other towns of the Plain and Coast, the climate of which, during the hot season, becomes almost unendurably hot.

Ootacamund is approached from the Plains by four ghauts, the Coonoor, Kotagherry, Seegoor, and Neddiwuttum or Goodaloor ghauts, on the slopes of some of which lie many large and valuable Coffee Estates.

Labour is not abundant, but many facilities, such as good roads, a magnificent climate, and a rich soil, render coffee cultivation on the Neilgherries a highly profitable as well as pleasant occupation.

Coffee is cultivated at a greater elevation in the Neilgherry Hills than in any other district, some estates there reaching as high as 6,000 feet above the sea; this would probably, in some seasons, be nearly the limit of frost.

The chief port of curing and shipment for the coffee produced in this district is Calicut, from which 30 miles or so of water carriage are available.

MYSORE AND MUNZERABAD.

COFFEE is supposed to have been naturalized in this country from 200 to 400 years, having been brought from Arabia by a pilgrim named Baba Booden, who established himself and a monastery near Chickmoogloor in the uninhabited hills named after him. It is most probable that from this origin sprung the coffee found growing in Coorg and other districts, before its cultivation was commenced by European planters.

More than 30 years ago a few Europeans were engaged in Coffee planting in Mysore, and the district called Munzerabad was established some 10 years later.

The port of shipment is Mangalore.

COORG.

COORG is a district some 60 miles in diameter, situated above the ghauts to the south of Mysore.

It is a native dependency under the Government of India, and is administered by a Superintendent appointed by the Supreme Government at Calcutta.

Its capital, Mercara, called by the natives "Mudkerry,"

is situated about 4,500 feet above the sea-level, and contains a Travellers' Bungalow, several private residences, and a fort garrisoned by a regiment of M. N. I., Protestant and Roman Catholic churches, and a very considerable bazaar, besides some European shops.

This town being situated on the summit of a mountain, is approached by three very excellent ghauts, one from the Coast at Tellicherry and Cannanore, which are about 50 miles distant, viâ Veerajenderpett; another from Mangalore, also distant about fifty miles; and the third from Mysore.

In the vicinity of Mercara are several Coffee Estates, some upwards of twenty years old, and on the Mangalore ghaut, some eight or nine miles from the town, lie some of the most promising and well-conducted estates I have ever seen, to the extent of some thousands of acres under cultivation. Fresh land is continually being opened, and is rapidly increasing in value.

The labour is drawn from Mysore, as in Wynaad and the Neilgherries, but the rate of pay is lower, being only 6 Rupees per mensem for men; notwithstanding which, the Canarese prefer this district, probably owing to the great abundance and cheapness of food.

The lower parts of this district consist of Bamboo jungle intermingled with forest trees, while the higher hills are covered with a dense and luxuriant forest. The soil is generally rich and fertile.

Veerajenderpett is the chief village in the lowlands, and its market is of considerable importance; it promises to become a place of note shortly from the number of planters who have settled themselves in its vicinity, and I have even heard rumours of the probable establishment of a Bank in the place, which would be an immense convenience to the planters of Coorg and a portion of Wynaad and Mysore, who are expending large sums in the cultivation of coffee.

The natives of Coorg are a fine, spirited, and athletic race, generally supposed to entertain a friendly feeling towards the English Government, to whom they rendered much assistance in the subjugation of Mysore.

The annual rainfall in Coorg is very great, being about 150 inches.

SHEVAROY HILLS.

The coffee plant was introduced into the Shevaroy Hills about the year 1820, by a Mr. Cockburn; notwithstanding this, I am given to understand that cultivation in that district is still in a backward condition—weeds being rampant, and pruning but little attempted. Under these circumstances, it cannot be wondered at that the average yield is not large.

Dr. Shortt, one of the residents, informs us that there are about 5,000 acres under cultivation of coffee.

The town of Salem, containing, I believe, about 40,000 inhabitants, is situated at the foot of these hills, and as the Madras Railway runs past the town, great facilities are afforded for extensive cultivation, both as to labor and transit.

The soil in the forest parts appears to be naturally rich, and land may be had from Government for the purposes of cultivation, on the annual payment of a rent of one Rupee per acre.

CHAPTER III.

TERMS FOR, AND MEANS OF PROCURING SUITABLE LAND IN CEYLON AND SOUTHERN INDIA.

To the intending cultivator, it may be useful, if I give some information as to the terms, on which land suitable for the cultivation of coffee, may be procured, in the districts of which I have endeavoured in the preceding chapter, to give some slight description.

In Ceylon, "waste lands" can be obtained from Government, on application to the Agent of the district or province, in which they are situated, and within a reasonable time from receipt of this, the extent within the boundaries or limits mentioned in the application, will be surveyed.

Should the block of forest be contiguous to grass land or Patnas, a certain portion of this will probably be included with the more desirable forest, and the whole will be advertised in the Government Gazette, with the name of the applicant, and in the newspapers, for sale by Public Auction, on such a day, at the Cutcherry of the district. The upset price for forest land is £1 per acre, though so valuable has land now become in Ceylon that one or two large blocks have been recently sold at £6.*

---

* In Happootella.

The purchaser becomes a freehold tenant, and the land is subject to no tax, or restriction.

These are by no means hard terms, in a country where the Government has, by a liberal and energetic policy, both as to public roads and bridges, and protective legislation, rendered the land really and permanently valuable.

In Wynaad, the state of the case is widely different; without roads, bridges or adequate ferries, in a country which a few days' rain render absolutely untraversable,* and which being inaccessible to wheeled traffic from or to the Coast, affords no easy means to its planters of removing their valuable and dearly bought produce. Where also the planter has no " labor ordinance" to protect him in the employment of a capricious and dishonest native population, all of which disadvantages render the soil less valuable, and the *prospects* of cultivation less secure, notwithstanding which the Government has rendered the attainment of land more difficult and dilatory, and the terms more complicated.

In this district application must be made to the Collector, at the same time naming the streams, paddy fields or other boundaries of the land required: after this, it is probable,

---

* In the monsoon of 1864, the tappals were prevented from reaching Manantoddy for fourteen days, by the flooding of the river, the raft or "pandy" having been washed away, and traffic entirely shut out on the Culputty side. At this date (July 4th) early in the monsoon, no tappal has been able to get in for five days from the same cause. Were the tappals to run from Tellicherry, no such stoppage could take place, as there is no river between Manantoddy and that port which ever becomes impassable. It certainly does seem surprising that the Government does not take this matter into consideration: surely for such a large European community and native population, as that of Manantoddy and North Wynaad, a separate runner might be afforded.

that in the course of some six months, the applicant *may* receive an official communication, informing him that enquiries are being made as to its whereabouts, whether there are other claimants to its possession, &c. Perhaps in a year the block may actually be advertised in the *Malabar Gazette*, and some time later put up for sale at the Cutcherry.

The upset price is the cost of survey, but the land is subject to an annual tax of Rupees 2 per acre, it being optional to compound for this, by the payment of twenty-five years' tax, or Rs. 50 per acre, besides the cost of survey, and any additional sum to which competitors may have raised the bidding.

Under these circumstances, it is not surprising that but little land has been hitherto bought from the Government for coffee cultivation in Wynaad; a preferable, as well as a more prompt and cheaper course, is to purchase land from natives, some of whom possess large tracts; the price asked latterly is about Rs. 10 per acre. Land thus purchased is free of tax, until it is cultivated, when the Government claim Rs. 2 per acre on all such part as has been brought into full bearing. Corresponding to this impost, but more equally distributed, a duty is levied in Ceylon, of one shilling per cwt. on all coffee exported.

In Coorg, the Government's terms for the sale of wastelands are most favorable to the man of small means. Applications are made to the Superintendent, naming the estimated area, situation, and boundaries of the lot desired, and the estimated cost of survey is deposited, (unless the land has already been surveyed,) any surplus of which will subsequently be re-funded; the Superintendent will now order the area to be estimated by the Talook authorities, and then advertise the lot for sale on a given day in English and Canarese, and have the notice of such sale posted for three months on the land itself and in the neighbourhood, and at the public offices.

The upset price is two Rupees per acre, to include all survey expenses: on the day fixed, the lot will be put up for sale by public auction, and sold to the highest bidder above the upset price, subject to an annual assessment *after four years*, of one Rupees per acre, and *after* (9) *nine years*, of Rupees two per acre, on the whole area, in perpetuance.

In order to make the payment easy for even the smallest capitalist, the successful bidder shall, on the day of sale, pay down 10 per cent. of the price, and the remainder within 30 days, *failing which, i. e.,* "If the purchase shall not be completed by the 30th day from the day of sale, the purchaser shall pay to the Superintendent interest at the rate of 12 per cent. per annum, on the remainder of his purchase money from the day of sale, until the purchase shall be completed, without prejudice, nevertheless, to the right of re-sale, if not paid *within one year.*"

Up to within a short time ago the Coorg Government made free grants of land, subject only to a restriction that a certain portion should be under cultivation within a specified time, and that then the valuable timber, as estimated by an official, on such portion, should be paid for at a nominal valuation.

CHAPTER IV.

ELEVATION, LAY, SITE, TEMPERATURE, ASPECT AND SOILS.

THAT coffee will not refuse to grow and even bear crop, in countries which are assailed by frost and snow, is proved by the following narrative from Dr. Willich's Encyclopædia, on the authenticity of which, he says the reader may fully rely :—" A nobleman in Germany found, in a bag of raw coffee, twenty green berries, resembling oblong cherries, and each of which contained two beans. In March, 1788, he planted them in a common garden-bed, two inches deep. In April it snowed, and was so cold, that the windows were covered with ice for two days. Notwithstanding this unfavorable prospect, five of the berries appeared above ground, in the latter part of June, and all the rest previous to the middle of July. They grew rapidly, being in a shady situation, and a soil somewhat sandy, but well manured. In September of the same year, they had attained a height of about six inches, and dropped their small leaves during Michaelmas. During the winter he covered them with a little hay, and afterwards with snow ; both of which were removed in the fine weather of April. In this simple manner, they were defended against the severity of German winters, and in the fifth year, four of the little trees, produced together seventy-six berries. By the inattention of the gardener, two of the plants died in the very hard frosts of 1798; yet the remaining eighteen were all in full blossom the ensuing spring, and yielded, in autumn, three pounds and a half of coffee berries; the flavour of which was not inferior to that imported from the island of Martinico."

Thus it is evident that extreme warmth is not absolutely necessary to the existence of the plant, but our object is to cultivate it in a climate where it will not only live, but flourish and bring forth fruit abundantly; experience shows that this is only the case within the tropics.

In Southern India and Ceylon, the elevation at which the estates are situated varies considerably; some are found having portions extending to nearly 6,000 feet above the sea, while others are as low as 300 or 400 feet. Where so much diversity exists, it is obviously difficult to give a decided opinion as to the exact elevation which is most suitable; the more so, as any traveller visiting those places, will have seen coffee trees growing, and bearing abundant crops, on the Sea Coast, at Colombo, Madras, Tellicherry, Calicut, &c.* In these instances, however, the trees are in the vicinity of native houses, and are probably well watered in the dry season, and I may, I believe, safely assert that the excessive drought, which in such climates, prevails for several months every year, would quite preclude the possibility of forming coffee estates at the sea level, unless, indeed, irrigation might, in some degree, remove the difficulty.

---

* I believe that when Coffee planters commenced operations in Ceylon, about 40 years ago, they first tried the low country, about Point de Galle, but soon abandoned it for the Hills.

In the district of Cornegalle, in Ceylon, there are several valuable estates having fields as low as 400 or 500 feet; in the Kaigalle district there are some between 500 and 1,000 feet, and in the neighbourhood of Kandy, in the Doombera valley, lie some well known plantations which are under certain circumstances, the most heavily yielding in that island. But estates at these low elevations are subject to the very serious drawback before alluded to, want of sufficient moisture, and a dry season will affect them so seriously, as occasionally to prevent the trees bringing their crops to maturity, and even to kill many of them.

It was owing to this fact that works for irrigating the Rajahwella estates, before alluded, were some years ago erected, at the enormous expense of between £14,000 and £15,000, which outlay has been productive of the most highly remunerative results.

It has been ascertained that coffee requires a great deal of moisture ; and a humid atmosphere, combined with a warm temperature, will tend to produce the most heavily-bearing trees ; but the latter requirement must not be overlooked, as it is well known, that on very elevated estates, where an almost perpetual fog and frequent rains, give more than an adequate supply of moisture, but where, at the same time, the air is seldom warm, even when the sun shines brightly, the coffee trees though sometimes presenting a healthy and even luxurious appearance, if the situation be sheltered, bear but very little crop. Such situations also prove, in many cases, strongholds of the blight called the black bug. Hence, amongst experienced planters, few would advocate felling above 4,000 feet. There are, nevertheless, exceptions to this rule; one estate in the Cotmalie district in Ceylon, and one in the Neilgherries, the former at 5,000 feet and the latter at nearly 6,000, forming the most notable I can at present call to mind; this is, probably, owing to some peculiar circumstances connected with the aspect or unusually good soil of these estates.

It is supposed to be partly owing to the great elevation of some of the districts of Ceylon, that the average yield of the whole island is so low as $5\frac{1}{2}$ cwt. per acre, the rate of produce in the districts of lower Hewahettie, Matella, Kallibokka, Knuckles, Rangalla, &c., being undoubtedly much higher. The elevation of most of the estates in the five districts named, ranges between 2,000 and 3,800 feet above the sea level; this forms good ground for assuming that at this height will be found more of the requisites of climate and temperature than at any other.

In elevations below 2,000 feet, a new obstacle presents itself, in that the great heat of the climate causes so rapid a growth of vegetation, that it is extremely difficult to keep down the weeds; this is so much the case, that whereas in some districts, at a tolerable elevation, one monthly weeding would be amply sufficient to keep an estate clean, in another, two would be quite necessary,* and in these days of scarcity of labour, this is a great drawback, the more so, that estates situated low are generally subject to malaria, a condition of the atmosphere, which, though suited to the coffee plant, is not conducive to human health.

The life of a Coffee planter has thus one vast superiority

---

* Such a district as Cotmalie, in Ceylon, is an instance of the former case, and Coruegalle, of the latter.

over most other vocations within the tropics, that his lot is from expediency, generally cast in a cool and agreeable climate, so that he is enabled to take that continued and fatiguing out-door exercise which his position calls for, which tends, doubtless, to render him the robust, manly, and genial being he is generally found to be. The temperature within the tropics at an elevation of 3,000 feet is, generally speaking, exceedingly mild and pleasant, exertion is not distressing, nor does a European suffer from that depressing langour, induced by the greater heat of the plains. English flowers and vegetables succeed well at such an elevation.

During the months of January, February, and March, the mornings and evenings are very cold and invigorating, but the noonday sun is, on the contrary, the hottest of the year. In this season but little rain falls, and the thermometer ranges between 70° and 80° in the shade at noon, in the sun it will rise to 125°. April and May are also pleasant months, though the occasional showers and thunderstorms, which now precede the advent of the monsoon, make it less healthy, though they tend to revive and freshen the aspect of nature, which, towards the end of the dry season, had become rather burnt up and exhausted. These thunderstorms set in generally in the end of April and in May, and usually occur in the afternoons after mornings of hot sunshine, causing a great evaporation of miasma and unhealthy gases from the ground, which are displayed in numerous cases of fever and dysentery among the coolies and others who by a low diet are particularly liable to such influences.

In the early part of June, and, indeed, for some time previously, heavy masses of clouds begin daily to gather up in the south-west horizon, fitful squalls and gusts of wind set in from the same direction, and then a day or two of driving mist, with some angry thunder crashes, usher in the burst of the monsoon, the great atmospheric event of the climate. Sheets of rain now fall with a vehemence and determination unknown in more temperate latitudes; violent winds roar through the forest, the sky is overcast with a perpetual curtain, and the climate is completely metamorphosed: with slight intervals of less inclement weather, the state of things lasts till the 1st of August, when pleasant breaks of sunshine cause nature to smile, after the beneficial, though apparently severe ordeal, and towards the end of August the weather of May commences again, and a condition of the atmosphere more suited to our imaginings of a tropical clime again resumes its sway.

In selecting a SITE for a plantation, there are so many subjects to be considered, so many evils to be avoided, that it would appear an almost hopeless task to pitch upon one entirely suitable. To make up, therefore, for natural deficiencies, additional attention is called for, to what may be denominated, the *science of coffee cultivation*.

As a guide to the inexperienced planter, I shall commence by enumerating some of the most important points to be observed in making a choice.

Whatever disadvantages or drawbacks it may sometimes be expedient to overlook, there is one which should, in all cases, be scrupulously avoided, and that is, a *bleak*, or *exposed situation*; for, though we can obviate many evils, a cold biting atmosphere and high unruly winds are giants which the art of man can only shun, not curb. The south-west monsoon wind, which blows incessantly for three or four months, is an ordeal, which a coffee estate fully exposed to its influence, cannot withstand. I have seen large fields of coffee abandoned in despair, after years of expensive attention, and assuredly if the planter has been so unfortunate as to have fixed on an aspect exposed to this influence, he will find it a profitless investment of capital.

Wind injures the plants in various ways; in some cases its effects are at once recognizable in the pinched, stunted, and almost frost-bitten appearance of the coffee plants, both as to wood and leaves, the former being hard and small, having, if I may use the expression, a precocious look, the latter crumpled also small, and tipped with yellow. In other cases the trees will be found denuded and shorn of leaves, on the side on which they are most assailed, forming on the opposite one, a growth more like that of the bushy hard Box-wood of cold climates.

In some cases, the wind acts with a different, though scarcely less fatal result, as in situations, where, by excessive moisture, or from other causes, the soil is rendered very soft and yielding, it does not denude the trees of leaves, but works the stem so much in the ground, that in a short time, a funnel is formed round the throat of the plant, the sides of which, continually chafing against the bark, wear it off, and the plant dies. A plant thus affected, is said to be "wind-wrung." Should it, however, be rescued before the bark is entirely worn off, the plant will generally recover, but its growth will be found seriously retarded.

In all the above cases, plants so injured, become extremely liable to be attacked by bug, worm, or any other blight, peculiar to the locality. In windy situations, however, precautionary and partially remedial measures may be adopted, which I shall subsequently describe : these are the more necessary, as when the block is far inland, it is not always possible to ascertain from its aspect, whether it is sheltered from certain winds or not ; indeed, a very small clearing of the forest lying adjacent will occasionally alter the direction of the wind so much, that it only remains to remedy what could not be foreseen. Thus I have known an estate which for many years remained quite sheltered, suddenly seriously injured by the different direction given to the wind by the felling of a belt of jungle, on a neighbouring estate, or the formation of a contiguous new clearing.

That wind should prove injurious to coffee cultivation, is not, however, surprising, as it is found to be the enemy of almost all vegetation. There are a few persons who have not at one time or other seen the farmer's crops laid low, from this cause, and it is a well ascertained fact that grass, though Nature's universal carpet, unless it be of a certain kind, does not flourish when exposed to it. Forming the only exception I know of, to this rule, is the Doombegas tree of Ceylon, which, it is said, flourishes best in situations where the atmosphere is habitually the most boisterous ; its abundance or otherwise is therefore not a bad criterion as to whether the land is sheltered or no.

There are vast tracts of the finest forest, in the high lands of Ceylon and all along the tops of the Western ghauts of India, which would be doubtless admirably adapted for the cultivation of coffee, tea, cinchona, and perhaps many other valuable products, but which will probably never be disturbed, owing to their being subjected to the onslaughts of the monsoon.

I have no doubt in my own mind, that this is one of those wise arrangements which an advancing science is daily discovering, and is calculated to preserve that moisture of the climate, which is necessary for the sustenance and welfare of the inhabitants. There is, I believe, little doubt that the cutting down of large tracts of forest, in any country, tends to decrease its water supply, so that we may suppose, that if these forests were all felled and cleared, this excessive cultivation would prove its own destroyer, and the annual rainfall so much decrease, that the vegetation would be parched up by long seasons of drought.

So important has this subject appeared to the Government, that I believe a Scientific Commission was at one time appointed for its consideration, which has resulted in various measures, amongst which are, I understand, rules for the preservation of a certain quantity of standing forest in each district above a fixed elevation, and also orders, by which headmen of villages are obliged to plant and tend young trees, such as mangoes, jacks, &c., bordering the roads, which pass through their districts.

That a sheltered situation is one of the most important considerations in the selection of the site for a new coffee estate, I have, I trust, satisfactorily shown, and I will now proceed to another branch of my subject, namely, the most favorable *aspect*.

As I have endeavoured to describe the pernicious, not to say ruinous, effects of winds, and as the strongest and most continuous wind of these parts comes direct from the south-west, it will be at once palpable that this aspect is the worst that could be fixed upon; neither is it wise to choose one diametrically opposite, as this is subjected, for some months in the year, to the north-east monsoon.

Northerly and easterly facings are the best, as these are not subjected to any direct violent wind, and the latter gets the full rays of the morning sun, a circumstance to which experience attaches much importance. We all know how an English gardener loves a southern aspect : this is because the cold bleak wind in England comes from the north, and in these latitudes the corresponding blast comes from the south.

Those who have made the long sea voyage from Great Britain will not readily forget the cold gale south of the Cape, when the wild and disturbed sky, the biting air and groaning timbers, all gave evidence that they approached the confines of a region, cold, drear, and inhospitable. When, therefore, we consider that the south-west monsoon collects its forces in such a quarter, can we be surprised that its influence, on tropical exotic cultivation, should be injurious, even were its blasts more gentle.

The next point to be considered is, what is technically termed, the " Lay" of the land.

That there are many estates situated on surfaces, greatly differing from each other and all apparently attaining the same satisfactory results, as to productiveness, would at first sight appear to argue that this subject is unimportant, but a similar inference might be drawn that elevation was of slight consequence from the knowledge that some estates are situated at 1,000 feet above the sea, and some at 5,000, yet bearing equally good crops, but those who have read the foregoing pages will be convinced of the fallacy of this supposition. I will, therefore, give the reasons from which I deduce my arguments, and it will then be competent to the reader to form his own deductions.

Out of about 500 estates in Ceylon, it must necessarily happen that there exists every variety of "lay," and that some of these are eminently more productive than others, must doubtless be ascribed to favorable "lay," as well as to other peculiarities. Out of the many different appearances which the uneven surface of a mountainous district presents, I will describe some dispositions which appear to me to be the most favorable. Slopes are the general feature observable, they are to be recommended owing to their incapacity to retain any undue quantity of water, which would be calculated to render the soil sour and stiff; they are also favorable, as regards the quantity of decayed vegetable matter which the rains must periodically wash over them from the hills above, thereby naturally leaving on their surface many valuable ingredients of soil: but after the land has been cleared and cultivated, this liability to "wash" becomes a very serious drawback, as matter which might have been retained; when the surface was covered by a close and minute vegetation, would float off after it had been cleared and the soil disturbed. Thus, slopes, unless protected from "wash" by artificial means, become poorer and poorer when under cultivation.

A flat lying at the base of high hills naturally contains rich soil, more especially if the hills which command it be covered with forest, as the decayed leaves falling during ages on the surface above, are necessarily partially washed down and deposited on it, thereby forming a rich loam. There is also a great advantage attendant on this lay, that the soil thus gained, it keeps, and should there be sufficient declivity to prevent stagnation, it is the best that can be adopted. One will frequently find a tolerably level stretch of land lying on the banks of some mountain stream, this would be particularly advantageous, as the superfluous moisture would thus be drained off, obviating any danger of the stagnation before-mentioned. Swampiness is a contingency which would prove quite fatal to coffee, and a sour soil in wet weather will generally be hard and impervious in the dry season, under which circumstances a coffee plant would soon die.

An estate forming two sides of valley, unless the outlet faced the unfavorable aspects before described, would promise well, as each side would protect the other, from the wind and the stream which would probably flow between, might be easily made available for curing operations.

One property with which I was acquainted, consisted of a number of knolls, or mounds, rising from the foot of a slope, and its extraordinary fecundity was ascribed to this remarkable conformation, the soil being thereby rendered perfectly sweet and friable.

To sum up, I may remark, that from my own experience, I would recommend, as a general rule, that preference be given to moderate slopes, towards the base of a range of hills, intersected by numerous ravines, or nullahs, with running streams, not only from the fact, that such a "lay" is entirely suitable, for the reasons above given, but also

. because it generally is not difficult to procure, in countries whose scenery is possessed of a mountainous character. But it must always be recollected that steep declivities are, if possible to be avoided, and that a slope as gradual and gentle as possible, is preferable to a perfectly flat block.

CHAPTER V.

SOIL.

Soil is a subject which admits of a great deal of discussion, though it is one which need not be made a primary point by persons who cultivate so great an extent of land as a coffee estate of ordinary dimensions necessarily covers·

A good plain axiom is, that when the soil is dark in color and free from grit, it is rich, and, therefore, good for coffee, as for most other cultivated plants.

Planters managing a heavily yielding estate, possessing a light red or yellowish soil, are apt to argue in favor of that particular colour; others may have come most in contact with black soil, others with that of a chocolate colour. But in making a choice of land, the best criterion is the luxuriousness or otherwise, of the vegetation on it, in its original state; for instance, in forests which have a thick under-growth, and which abound in creepers and mosses, it may be safely concluded that the soil is good.

In making an excavation in land, it will generally be perceived that the first stratum is dark in color, and that the shade lightens as we proceed in depth, until it gradually becomes a yellowish composition of sand and clay; and the thickness of the upper stratum, or real soil, is the guage of the probable productiveness of the land.

To the practical cultivator on a large scale, a knowledge of the chemical constituents of soils is rarely necessary, but as a few remarks on soils generally may be found useful, I extract the following, which may be easy of retention and application, from Mr. Loudon's work on gardening:—

"*The leading soils for the cultivator* are the clayey, calcareous, sandy, ferruginous, peaty, saline, moist or aquatic, and dry. *Plants are the most certain indicators of the nature of a soil :* for while no practical cultivator would engage with land of which he knew only the results of a chemical analysis or examined by the sight and touch, * * * yet every one who knew the sort of plants it produced, would be at once able to decide as to its value for cultivation.

"Earths, exclusively of organized matter and water, are allowed by most physiologists, to be of no other use to plants, but that of supporting them, or furnishing a medium by which they may fix themselves to the globe. But earths and organic matter, that is, soils, afford at once support and food.

"*The true nourishment of plants is water, and decomposing organic matter.*

"*The constituent parts of the soil which give tenacity and coherence, are finely divided matters ;* and they contain the power of giving those qualities in the highest degree, when they contain much alumina. A great proportion of sand, however, always produces sterility. * * * *

"Vegetable or animal matters, when finely divided, not only give coherence, but likewise softness and penetrability: but neither they, nor any other part of the soil must be in too great proportion.

"*A certain degree of friability, or looseness of texture,* is also required in soils, in order that the operations of culture may be easily conducted; that moisture may have free access to the fibres of the roots; that heat may be readily conveyed to them; and that evaporation may proceed without obstruction. These are commonly obtained by the presence of sand.

"As alumina possesses all the properties of adhesiveness, in an eminent degree, and silex those of friability, it is obvious that a mixture of these two earths, would furnish everything wanted to form the most perfect soil, as to water and the operations of culture.

"The power of soil to absorb water from air, is much connected with fertility; when this power is great, the plant is supplied with moisture in dry seasons. * * * * The soils most efficient in supplying the plant with water, by atmospheric absorption, are those in which there is a due mixture of sand finely divided clay, and carbonate of lime, with some animal or vegetable matter, and which are so loose and light, as to be freely permeable to the atmosphere. *The absorbent power of soils, is always the greatest in the most fertile.*

"The absorption ought to be much greater in WARM OR DRY COUNTRIES. Soils also on declivities ought to be more absorbent than in plains, or in the bottoms of valleys.

"Their productiveness is likewise influenced by the nature of the subsoil, or the stratum on which they rest. When soils are immediately situated on a bed of rock, they are much sooner rendered dry by evaporation, than when the subsoil is of clay or mud. A clayey subsoil will sometimes be of material advantage to a sandy soil. A sandy or gravelly subsoil, often corrects the imperfections of too great a degree of absorbent power in the true soil.

"Stagnant water may be considered as *injurious to all land plants*, by obstructing perspiration, and thus diseasing their roots and submerged parts."

I think we may gather from the foregoing quotation, first, that luxuriant vegetation is a sign of rich soil; and also, that the natural growth of certain plants may indicate the character of its constituent parts; might we not go a step further and say, that in selecting a soil adapted for the growth of coffee, it would be wise, as doubtless practicable, to observe closely the nature of the growth on land adjacent to some already made and heavily yielding coffee estate; this peculiarity might be used as a guide in our choice, as other land producing the same kind of plants, would doubtless be equally suitable.

Fine and rich soil must contain suitably admixed proportions of earths, moisture, and decomposing organic matter; these characteristics will afford nutriment.

The next requirement is, the due degrees of the qualities of adhesiveness, friability, and *power of absorption*, the latter being especially important, in hot or dry climates.

It may, in addition, be observed that as one of the largest constituents of coffee is phosphate of lime; a soil containing much of this property, would be the most fruitful, and eminently suited to the coffee planter.

CHAPTER VI.

OPENING, COOLIES, TOOLS.

In opening a new estate, the first undertaking will be the obtaining a gang of laborers. The next the purchase of a supply of tools.

Unlike most other countries, and, especially, unlike our own mother-country, India presents great difficulties in the way of procuring the first desideratum.

This fact is doubtless, as I said before, ascribable to the lethargic and slothful character of the Asiatic of the lower orders, and to the cheapness of food. I saw it stated the other day, that in 1826, it was calculated, that in the Bombay Presidency, a family of five persons, could live comfortably for one month, on a sum not exceeding two Rupees, eight Annas; or five shillings—about one shilling a head, per month. This is doubtless not the case now, but still, I have calculated that a cooly in Ceylon can feed and clothe himself comfortably on two-thirds of his monthly wages, and a Canarese coolie in India, on less than one-third.

Under these circumstances, it is hardly surprising that coolies are scarcely procurable in sufficient quantities, or that when they engage themselves, they only work for short periods. They have no ambition, as a rule no desire for wealth, so that their wants from day to day are satisfied, they desire no more. What inducement have they then to offer themselves for hard work ? At present, such inducements as there are, are insufficient.

To get a gang of men, the first step to be taken is to engage the services of a cangany, maistry, or duffadar ; this can generally be done by the assistance of some planting friend, if not, employment may be offered to a native writer or Conductor on condition that he bring in a gang of coolies.

An advance of a sum of money must be given him, to enable him to do this : but before giving him this advance, it will be highly advisable to obtain some security from him for its re-payment.

When we consider the mendacity and general dishonesty, (especially in small things) of all uncivilized and uneducated people, more especially those of the lowest ranks, and the poverty which would naturally induce a man, whose sole worldly possessions were displayed on his person, to make away with a (large to him) sum of money intrusted to his care ; it appears almost incredible that the advance system, carried on as it is, should be practised, or when practised, succeed in any case. It requires however a very short residence in India, to shew one, that as things stand, it is absolutely necessary. Should you require a pair of boots, the " chackler" must have an advance before he sets to work on them ; a coat, and the tailor prefers the same request, and yet the more we consider the subject the more iniquitous it must appear. In nine cases out of ten if the person under advance chooses to abscond, he is beyond the reach of detection. Suppose a planter in Ceylon to give Mootoosamy Cangany, (probably Mootoosamy is a horsekeeper out of employment, who has invested his last rupee in the purchase of an umbrella and a walking stick as the insignia of his new dignity,) £10 to go to the coast to get him a gang of coolies, Mootoosamy will doubtless proceed to the coast, but will he return with coolies ? Most probably not, the £10 will have raised him to dignity and affluence in his native village, and the deluded planter will expect his return in vain. Then when conviction flashes upon his mind, let him try and catch Mootoosamy, where is the delinquent ?—echo answers " where ?"

What purpose is the advance system intended to serve ? Is it as a guarantee to the poor ignorant native, that the Sahib-logue will not swindle him out of his just remuneration ? I do not believe that, as a rule, the natives of India are afraid of this contingency, precedent shews them that such a supposition is absurd.

There are, doubtless, cases where natives are so poor as to be unable to undertake works of a certain class, without an advance of money, to enable them to buy material. But I need hardly ask my reader, whether these are the only circumstances under which advances are given ?

And so it is in procuring labourers ; the maistry must receive an advance to enable him to advance part of their pay to the coolies he engages. The maistry in question may probably have earned sufficient during previous service to have rendered him a wealthy man, for his class, and most likely he is quite in a position if he wished it, to make the coolie advances out of his own spare cash ; but, nevertheless, the advance must be forthcoming, and all the while the person who receives it, to use as much for his own benefit as for the planter's has Rupees galore buried in some quiet nook at home.

Canganies in Ceylon often receive £20, £30, or even £50 in this manner. It will be supposed that large sums are often lost, and so they are in cases where the cangany is a new hand, but in the majority of cases, where he has earned some confidence from his master during lengthened service, some of his friends give security for his return, or else his family remains at work on the estate as it were in pledge, so that losses are not so frequent as might be expected. Care is needful in the selection of the persons to whom money is to be entrusted, in this way, as they are sometimes apt to expend the greater part of the sum for their own benefit, extorting from their coolies exorbitant interest for the moiety given them, so as to repay their master the whole amount. This circumstance in many cases has been the cause of coolies absconding from estates, merely to escape from their remorseless and usurious creditor the cangany, while the manager probably has attributed their desertion, being probably guided himself by the cangany's representations, to totally different causes.

Contract labor where available should always have preference, since it saves supervision and anxiety. In Ceylon, no difficulty is experienced in obtaining trustworthy and competent contractors to undertake felling, clearing and burning, building lines, &c., who only require to be supplied with tools, and rice for the consumption of their men.

These contracts are, for the most part, verbal, and advances are seldom given on the work until it is commenced. The usual plan is, to pay so much per acre after the felling is completed, and the balance on the clearing being handed over ready for culture.

In India, the system is more abstruse, a written contract being there entered into on *stamped paper*, signed in the presence of witnesses, and an advance of part payment made, in order to render the agreement binding. In making these agreements, there are several points to be attended to, to render them valid.

It is necessary to state the amount of work; the rate of remuneration agreed on; the date when the work is to be commenced; by what day it is to be completed; and the amount of advance.

I believe, without an advance, no contract to perform work is binding, by the Indian law.

The value of the stamp is to be proportioned to the amount of the advance, and not of the work to be performed.

These formalities having been properly complied with, a breach of contract is considered criminal, and punishable by imprisonment, &c.

Unfortunately, however, contracts, as a system, cannot be said to succeed in India, at least as far as my Wynaad experiences go. Although surprising, it is no less true that almost any native will agree, and bind himself to perform any sort of work, under whatever penalty, without the slightest hesitation or compunction, provided the amount of the advance, which by law *must* be given, be sufficient to gratify a momentary desire, or stave off a present difficulty.

To give success to a system of contracts, it should be necessary for contractors to give some material guarantee of fulfilment; natives cannot in most cases do this, and Europeans in contracting to get work performed, will not, because they themselves are liable to suffer from the very vicissitudes in labour, which the contract system is intended to alleviate.

In getting coolies, no Planter is in a position sufficiently independent, to select the exact class of men he wishes to employ; the first who come, and all who come, are generally gladly received: were this not so, the following remark from Dr. Shortt's recent work, might doubtless be applied with advantage:—" In the employment of coolies, powerful and healthy men, if possible from among the hill tribes, should be selected, if any be procurable in the vicinity, as they are the most expert in the use of the axe." Another reason and an important one, why mountaineers should be preferred, is that coffee estates being always in mountainous districts, they would not have to experience such a change of climate and temperature as would be likely to disagree with them.

Tools are instruments which are used in performing mechanical operations on soils or other substances; in the present case with reference to the destruction or cultivation of plants, or vegetation: those necessary for the working and formation of a coffee estate are of various kinds, and as they are mostly of a different form and character from those in general use in gardening operations in Europe, I will proceed to give some description of the most necessary.

Tools should always be made of metal of the best description; of wrought iron with edges of cast steel, and, if possible, of the most approved shapes and size.

There is an adage to the effect that "bad workmen make bad tools," but one equally true might be composed, with reference to bad tools spoiling good workmen. Good implements also, are more economical, as they last longer; therefore, though they are more expensive, I would always advocate the purchase of the best that can be had.

"Mammoties" are a kind of heavy, short-handled, hoe, like an English mattock; they should have handles three feet or three and a half feet long; if required for digging, the blade should be heavy and strong, six inches wide and about nine inches long, from the eye to the edge; if for surface scraping, weeding, or shovelling loose earth or sand, they may be ten inches wide by nine deep. Mammoties are used for any purpose for which a pick and shovel together, a shovel separately, or a spade would be applied in Europe. It is obvious, that for laborers who go barefoot, the latter instrument would be quite useless.

Billhooks, or "Barcatties." This instrument consists of a large blade for cutting under-growth, or lopping branches from felled trees, or for cutting and dressing any green wood, too small to be operated on by the axe, and not requiring the accuracy of the saw; it is sometimes sharpened on one, sometimes on both sides.

It may either have a handle three or four feet long or six inches, at the option of the laborer, or according to the description of work for which it is required.

The billhook in common use among the Cingalese has a handle about four feet in length, is sharpened on one side only, and is much hooked in the blade: that used by the local tribes of Malabar, is similarly shaped as to the blade, but with a short handle.

The best form for all purposes, is a heavy blade nine inches in length, sharpened on one side, with an iron socket handle, into which a wooden haft can be inserted at pleasure.

The axes most commonly used for felling, are long and narrow, as to the blade, having a round eye for the insertion of the handle; those made in the English manner for square-headed handles, being troublesome to fit. A curious description of the axe in use amongst the natives of Malabar, is a wedge of iron, thrust into an iron-bound helve: but this axe is troublesome, being composed of so many different parts, *i.e.*, the wedge-shaped blade, the handle, and the two binding rings. Axes for the planter should be of better material than ordinary, as many of the trees to be felled are of such very hard material that inferior axes break up in a very short time.

The crowbar should be flattened at one end, and pointed at the other; it is useful as a lever for taking out stones, removing heavy weights, loosening the earth, and cutting roots, in narrow pits which require depth.

"Quintannies" or mattocks, will be found most useful where the ground to be dug is hard or gravelly; they should be sharp and heavy, the blade five inches by ten.

A few grass hooks, or sickles, and some pickaxes similar to those in use in England, a grind stone, and some other few instruments which require no description, make up the list.

Having procured a *gang of coolies*, and a proper *supply of tools*, the first work to be undertaken, is the erection of houses for the planter and his men. For this purpose, a small piece of land should be cleared first—this spot should be carefully selected, and the following advantages be looked to; a dry, healthy and moderately elevated situation; a good supply of water; and convenience as regards the future estate and the nearest public road.

In making a clearing, the underwood and saplings must first be cut down by a party of men (or boys) armed with billhooks; these should be followed by the axe men to cut down the large trees. Should the position be determined upon for the future permanent bungalow, it will be well to leave a few of the most picturesque and symmetrically formed trees standing, to add to the coolness and beauty of the spot. In felling trees, it is always well to consider that though two or three axe men can, in a few hours, bring down a fine old tree, having perhaps a growth of centuries, it is always impossible to repair the error, should the result prove a want of forethought and consideration.

Five or six weeks after the trees have been felled, the débris should be fired, and after the burn as much as necessary of the residue piled and re-kindled, to render the ground perfectly clear. Operations may now be commenced by the immediate erection of lines for the coolies; these may be run up in a very short space of time, from the material abundantly provided around by nature; next should be erected a temporary bungalow for the planter himself. It is a most important point, to provide the coolies with proper accommodation, and the planter should always remember, that though he may be ready to "rough it" himself, he will not find them so willing to do so. It is not, however, necessary to put up coolie lines, of an expensive or even permanent character, and this is seldom done on new estates; the great object being to exclusive eternal influences such as wind and rain, any building which thoroughly answers these requirements, will be sufficient.

In localities where the Bamboo flourishes, it is a simple and expeditious job to erect a house, and that in a manner which would surprise an artizan, in our own country, for in this case no nails are used, and, in fact, no material which is not entirely the production of the adjacent jungle. The principal supports of the house are usually not of bamboo, it being liable to destruction by weevils, though, indeed, if cut near the root, and then left to soak in water, a post of this description will last a long time.

When bamboos are required for building, the natives always cut them when the moon is on the decline, as when this is done the sap is not rising in the bamboos, and they are consequently less liable to premature decay.

The walls of houses are made of bamboo split into lathes and woven like basket-work, subsequently plastered with mud, to fill up the interstices. Several valuable descriptions of fibre, which abound in almost every locality, afford material for tying the roof; which latter, it is unnecessary to say, will consist of grass thatch.

Coolies' lines are generally simply one long building partitioned off into different habitations, each division about ten or twelve feet square, having a door communicating with the outside. Four or five persons will inhabit one room if it is tolerably large, and they are of the *same caste.* Married people should be provided with a room to each couple.

The Manager's temporary bungalow to be now built, will doubtless be a simple parallellogram, divided into three rooms, or even two, with a verandah along the front, each end of which can be enclosed, and used as a pantry and bath room.

A building of this kind may be made very comfortable, and if put up of good posts, or "wattle and dab," will stand for many years; this being the case, when a "puckah" Bungalow is subsequently erected, the original one may be used as godowns, cook-house, &c.

In districts where the felling *can* be performed by contract, the manager will be in a position comfortably to proceed with the above works, by means of his gang of daily paid coolies, while the contractors are going on with the felling; after the buildings are completed, a nursery should be made; that is to say, if plants are not abundant in the adjacent jungle, or to be cheaply purchased in the villages.

CHAPTER VII.

NURSERIES.

In Ceylon, in the vicinity of old Estates, abundant supplies of coffee plants of all sizes can generally be obtained in the forest, the result of the pillage of numerous tribes of monkeys, wild cats, squirrels, &c. Such plants, from having grown entirely in the shade, are lanky and delicate, but when cut off about six inches above the first feeding roots, they come on very well, and grow readily when planted into the estate: after this operation they are termed by planters "stumps."

The best size for selection, are those whose stem is rather thicker than a common lead pencil, as they bud and take root much more quickly than large ones, and those which are thinner are more delicate and are liable to be burnt up.

Where jungle plants are not to be had, any number may usually be purchased from the native owners of small coffee gardens at the rate of about 2s. or 2s. 6d. per 1,000.

Under either of the above circumstances, a nursery would be an unnecessary and wasteful undertaking, but should the planter not find himself so fortunate as to have plants thus provided for his use, it will be advisable to commence the formation of a nursery at once.

The time of year at which the planter should commence this work, is about the end of October; and at this time it will be easy to purchase a few bushels of fresh coffee for seed, from the firstlings of the crop on any of the adjacent estates.

A bushel contains about 40,000 berries of cherry coffee; thus, as each berry consists of two beans, it will be palpable that a bushel will contain at least 80,000 seeds: from this number it will be prudent to deduct 10 per cent. as non-germinating, and we then have a result of about 70,000 plants from one bushel of parchment coffee.

Seeds should be taken from perfectly healthy trees, of a good description, and when picked should be quite ripe; each berry should have the beans pressed out of it by hand, as, if passed through the pulpers, a certain number will be injured by the machinery: they should not be washed, but mixed with a quantity of wood-ashes, which will dissolve the saccharine pulp adhering to the beans, and prevent their fermenting; they should then be slightly dried, when they will be ready for use.

The seed-beds must be dug up to the depth of a foot, all roots and stones picked out, and the surface smoothed over. The coffee may then be put in, either broadcast or in drills, and *lightly* covered with a *sprinkling* of fine mould; over this should be placed a layer of rotten leaves, about two inches in depth, and the whole well watered *at least* once in every three days, until the seeds come up, which will occur in six weeks: if it be practicable to water every day, so much the better; when the seeds have come above ground, the layer of leaves must be gently removed.

The germination of the seed is thus most correctly described:—"Let the seed, with its parchment, be laid only upon a wet soil, you see it open itself a little. A pedicle peeps out, an extremity of which leans towards the ground. Here two radicals are seeking and soon grasp their nurse. The other extremity rears itself up, loaded with the whole seed. In a short time, two follicles, almost round, and of a thin yellow colour, unfold themselves from the very substance of the seed, and shake off the parchment. The stigma or fissure seemed to mark their separation on the flat side of the seed; and, on the round side, they seemed to be perfectly blended together; but now they part of themselves. Thus it is the seed itself which spreads out into these two follicles, which turn green by the contact of the air.

"From between them a small top rises. Its point is acute and divides itself into two leaves, of lanceolous form. The sappling rises again and again, still in the same manner, bearing its leaves two and two, or axillary, at equal distances, and every pair opposite to each other, above and below."

Dr. Shortt, in his work on Coffee, lately published, makes several very erroneous remarks in his instructions for the formation of a nursery. 1st.—"The land should be thoroughly ploughed up or trenched with the mammotie, to the depth of 18 or 24 inches * * *." This is clearly unnecessary, as the roots of the seed plant will never penetrate more than a foot in depth, *within the space of time they are likely to remain in the nursery.* I have never seen the ground dug up more than one foot, and this depth I consider ample.

2nd.—" When it should be freely manured, at the rate of 3 to 5 tons per acre." A nursery on a new estate, such as Dr. Shortt is describing, would be on virgin soil, in which case manure would not only be a waste, but absolutely detrimental to the seed.

3rd.—" The seeds should be the produce of trees from 7 to 10 years of age." I am of opinion that if the seed be well formed and ripened, the age of the tree from which they are obtained is quite immaterial.

4th.—He says, they should be sown " at a depth of one inch." This is a great mistake, if an early and forward nursery is desired, as in this case, they certainly will not germinate under 2 or 3 months.

5th.—They should be placed " in drills 10 or 12 inches apart from each other." If this plan be adopted, let the planter calculate what extent of land would be necessary for a nursery of two lacs (200,000) of plants, allowing 100 per cent. of space for paths, water channels, &c.

Lastly.—Dr. Shortt observes, seeds " seldom come up under three weeks or a month," this is not surprising, when we consider that six weeks is the time required in all ordinary cases.

While on the subject of nurseries, I must warn the planter, that if hand watering be resorted to, it should be done in the morning or evening, and not during the heat of the day, as the application of water when the sun is shining will produce so great an evaportion, as to cause a chill, and be fatal to the plants.

The beds should not be more than six feet wide or less, so that a person standing on either side may be able to reach the centre without removing his foot from the path. This is in order that weeds may be easily pulled out, or the beds watered without injury. They may be either raised above, the paths surrounding them, or otherwise, as each method has its advantages in different localities; in moist situations, the beds should be raised above the surface, for dryness; and in very dry hot localities, they should be depressed, so as to retain the moisture they receive.

Many planters of experience prefer to make them in the manner of a paddy field, that is to say, level, and below the bund, or path by which they are surrounded, so that a stream of water may be turned in on each when necessary. The disadvantage of this plan for a seed nursery is, that the rush of water is apt to disturb the seeds, and wash them into heaps.

After the plants are once up, however, this is the cheapest and most expeditious method of watering them, (where the soil is not inclined to clayeyness), and they may be flooded every other day.

If the nursery is intended as a seed-nursery only, it does not much matter how close the seeds lie; but if the young plants are intended to remain in it for a second season, they should be 3 or 4 inches apart every way, and put in drills at regular distances, so that it will always be easy to ascertain the number of plants in each bed, by measuring the space they occupy. Thus, in a bed 6 feet wide by 18 feet long, planted at 3 inches apart, there will be 1,750 plants.

In hot climates, it will be necessary, just as the seed is springing up, to erect a "Pandall" or shade over the nursery; this can be done in a very rough manner, the best covering for it being green branches out of the jungle. This Pandall should be removed on the approach of the rainy season, otherwise the drip will prove injurious; besides, the sun and air let in on the plants at this season will tend to render them hardy.

In the subsequent up-keep of the "Nursery" from year to year, the best method will be, to make fresh seed-beds, and when they are 4 or 5 months up, transplant them into the original nursery, which must be previously re-dug, and some new soil added, and, perhaps, a little rotten dung or compost, but *not too much manure*.

It appears probable that plants grown in very rich nurseries, would suffer from the change when planted out in rather poorer soil, and this is a strong argument against manuring nurseries. Some cultivators are of opinion, that the seeds should be sown in the same soil, in which the plants are subsequently to be grown, and that, therefore, plants brought from a nursery at a distance, would receive a considerable check when planted into the new estate.

CHAPTER VIII.

ON FELLING AND CLEARING.

THE appearance of a newly felled clearing in Ceylon is thus described:—" The sun was high in the horizon, when we found ourselves at a turn of road, in the midst of a clearing; the spot we had opened on, was at the entrance of a long valley, of great width, on one side of which lay the estate we were bound to. It was not difficult to fancy one's self in the recesses of the black forest, pile on pile of heavy, dark jungle, rose before us. Before us were, as near as I could judge, fifty acres of felled jungle in the thickest disorder; just as the monarchs of the forest had fallen, so they lay, heap upon heap, crushed and splintered into ten thousand fragments. To me it was a pretty as well as novel sight to watch the felling work in progress. Two axe men to each tree if small, three and sometimes four to larger ones: their little bright axes flung far back over their shoulders, and then dug deep into the heart of the tree. I observed that in no instance were the trees cut through, but each one was left with just sufficient of the heart to keep it standing. On looking round I saw that there were hundreds of them treated similarly; my planter-friend assured me, that if the trees were to be at once cut down, a few at a time, they would so encumber the ground, as to render it impossible for the workmen to have access to the adjoining trees. They (the workmen) were ranged in order; all being ready, forty bright axes gleamed high in the air, then sunk deeply into as many trees, which at once yielded to the sharp steel, groaned heavily, then toppled over, and fell with a stunning clash on the trees below them; these having been cut through previously, offered no resistance, but followed the example of their upper neighbours, and fell booming on those beneath. In this way, the work of destruction went on from row to row; only those fell, however, which had been cut, and of these not one was left standing."

Felling bamboos is a more laborious and tedious operation, this is done with the billhook.

The bamboo with which the whole of the interior of Wynaad abounds, is one of the most useful of plants. It grows in clusters scattered at irregular distances, sometimes over grass land, and sometimes interspersed with forest trees; in either case, it forms a beautiful feature in the landscape, giving it a soft and feathery appearance. It is universally used by the natives for building, for which purpose, from its length, strength, and straightness, it is peculiarly adapted: they also fashion from it receptacles for water or grain, buckets, bottles, and also spoons, baskets, mats, &c.

In the Shervaroy Hills, where it is not so plentiful, I am given to understand that the planters, when making clearings, do not fell the bamboos, reserving them for use as required. This fact I am at a loss to reconcile with the feeling of the Wynaad planters, that the close vicinity of bamboos to coffee is injurious; the correctness of which belief I am inclined to support.

In felling them, the thorny branches surrounding each clump have to be removed in detail, so as to leave a clear space of about six feet high, to enable the workman to make his attack on the stems. Each stem is then cut through about 5 feet from the ground, and again at the base, and the piece removed to afford access to those inside.

When all are cut through, the entire clump comes down, firmly bound together by its innumerable thorny branches. It is indispensable entirely to sever each stem, as a very slight connecting ligament will be sufficient to enable a prostrate bamboo to retain its vitality, which contingency will quite prevent its destruction when the torch is applied.

After the bamboos are down, any trees that may be standing about, are filled over them in order that by their great weight they may condense the piles already prostrate, with a view to the burn being more effectual.

After felling, " lopping" commences, that is to say, all branches which have an upward or straggling tendency are cut down, that they may lie as flat as possible. This work should be entered upon before the leaves have fallen, as this latter contingency would prove prejudicial to the prospects of a good burn, it would be better, in order to avoid any danger of this, to have a small gang lopping from the first, following a day or two behind the felling gang.

In about a month after felling, the clearing may be fired. To do this successfully, some precautions should be taken.

Should the clearing be on a hill side, the best plan is to

apply the torch in places about 70 or 80 yards apart from each other, in two or three lines across its face, commencing near the top. If on a flat, fires may be applied all round and in the centre. The burn should not commence till about 12 or 1 o'clock in the day, in order that the dews of the preceding night may have thoroughly evaporated.

Though a "good burn" is almost always desired by the planter, it is doubtful whether a fierce fire is not prejudicial to the soil, as it must calcine whatever decayed vegetable matter forms the first inch of the surface.

Were it practicable to get rid of the mass of timber and brushwood, without burning, I have no doubt it would be advantageous, but as this is not the case without an enormous expenditure of labour, a fire is the only resource for clearing the land.

There is no doubt, however, that the clearer the land is left, the greater facility the planter will find in planting it with neatness and regularity.

I have somewhere seen it recommended to pile the fallen timber and brushwood in rows, and leave it to decay, planting the coffee in the intervening spaces, but this is quite impracticable for many reasons, and, were it not so, nests of weed would thus be formed, which it would be impossible to eradicate.

Should the fire not have rendered the land sufficiently free of brushwood, clearing will have to be entered upon, and all superfluous branches and timber cut up, put into heaps, and re-fired.

So strong a feeling have some planters against the injury caused to the soil by burning clearings, that they have endeavoured to obviate it, by lining and pitting the land *before* felling, but as in this method the rows cannot be made with any straightness or exactitude, the work has afterwards a slovenly appearance, so that I cannot recommend it. I recollect once lending a friend of mine some of my spare labourers, to line and pit for him in an uncleared forest, but the coolies suffered so severely from the jungle leeches that they could not continue the work. These leeches are one of the greatest pests met with by the planter in the forest districts; frequenting all shady and damp situations, they attack every passer-by: they are smaller than the medicinal leech, and must have different qualities from it, as their bite is notoriously apt to fester, and create bad ulcers if irritated. To obviate this evil, the planters and others, whose avocations compel them to pass much time in the jungle, wear a kind of outside stocking made of linen, which is tied over the trousers below the knee. The best remedy for the acute itching and morbid inflammation caused by the bite of the jungle leech, is to rub in salt: failing relief, burn the part with caustic.

CHAPTER IX.

LINING, PITTING, AND FILLING.

With a view to affording facility for gangs of people, to work on an estate with order and quietness ; and that an estimate may be made of the amount of work performed by each person ; as well as to avoid any waste of surface, and to afford to each plant its due space for obtaining nourishment, every estate is " lined ;" that is to say, the spot for every plant is marked with a picket, and these pickets are placed at equal distances apart in perfectly straight lines throughout the plantation. This gives the estate an appearance of neatness and regularity, very pleasing to the eye.

The work is performed in the following manner : the pickets or " lining pegs" (of which a coolie will, in a day, make from 300 to 400) must be previously provided ; they should be about 3 feet long, and sufficiently strong to admit of their being well hammered into the ground without breaking : a rope must also be obtained, and divided into the distances intended to exist between the trees, by strips of calico ; and a couple of measuring wands in order to regulate the space to be left between each line.

The rope having been previously well stretched, the work can commence by its being held in a straight line in whatever direction is wished, the usual one being straight up the hill side, *i. e.*, " conforming as much as possible to the greatest declivity of the ground," and a peg should be driven into the ground at every mark on the rope. Two coolies, each provided with one of the measuring sticks before-mentioned, should then measure and plant pickets in a straight line, *rectangularly*, to the direction taken by the rope, at either end. When the first line is marked out, the rope must be moved to the next corresponding pickets, a parallel line marked, and so on. Care should be taken in measuring from line to line, that the stick be held perfectly level, as well as at right angles with the line, as, should this not be done, the real distance between the lines will be less, and the lines, instead of running parallel, will gradually converge.

Other and more complicated systems of lining are frequently adopted, but are more difficult and tedious of performance, with coolies. In order to line square, "or make right-angled lines," it is necessary to use three ropes, each marked with strips of calico, place two of them parallel at 50 or 60 yards apart, and the third hold from one to the other at the corresponding marks on each.

The distances between the marks on the rope should be frequently measured, and if they have increased by stretching, the marks re-adjusted.

In the West Indies, and also, I believe, in Java, the space left between each picket, is frequently 10 or 12 feet, this is never allowed in Ceylon or Southern India; the usual distances being 6 feet × 6 feet, or 6 feet × 5 feet, or 5 feet × 5 feet, or 5 feet × 4 feet, and very rarely wider than 6 feet.

The distance at which the pits should be dug, must, in a great measure, be decided by the nature of the soil, and climate ; the criterion appears to be, that while having the greatest possible number of trees in a given space, none shall interfere in the growth or sustenance of another. In cold or exposed situations, where the coffee trees do not attain any great size, they should be planted close : in warm humid climates where the soil is rich, 6 feet by 6 feet will be found suitable.

It is desirable that the foliage of the plants should touch, but not intertwine, in order that the cover thus made may check the growth of weeds, but it is not advisable that this cover should be of sufficient density, to exclude all the light or too much of the air from the soil. A space of 6 feet × 5 feet will suit almost any climate or soil.

An acre planted @ 6 feet × 6 feet will contain 1,210 plants
,,   ,,   ,,   @ 6 ,, × 5 ,,   ,,   ,,   1,452   ,,
,,   ,,   ,,   @ 5 ,, × 5 ,,   ,,   ,,   1,742   ,,
,,   ,,   ,,   @ 5 ,, × 4 ,,   ,,   ,,   2,178   ,,
,,   ,,   ,,   @ 4 ,, × 4 ,,   ,,   ,,   2,722   ,,

Another method of lining which may be adopted, is termed Quincunx, in which the plants in every *alternate* line are opposite to each other.

" It has been demonstrated *(Farmer's Magazine,* Vol. VII., 409,) that the closest order in which it is possible to place a number, upon a plain surface, not nearer than a given distance from each other, is in the angles of hexagons, with a plant in the centre of each hexagon. Hence it is argued that this order of trees is the most economical, as the same quantity of ground will contain a greater quantity of trees by 15 per cent., when planted in this form than in any other."*

Quincunx is not to be recommended to the coffee planter, as it will be found quite beyond the comprehension of the coolies, and hence a source of infinite delay, annoyance, and trouble. Moreover, from the ruggedness of the ground, in forest clearings, with large logs, stumps and boulders scattered in every direction, it will be impossible to preserve so exact a form ; " the advantage of which is to approximate the rows, and, of course, to gain ground, though the trees are still at the same respective distances. This method has the inconvenience of narrowing the passage for the laborers, and the boughs will suffer from it in the extremities. Besides, the gardeners of Europe have renounced Quincunxes because they intercept the free passage of air, which is necessary to the trees." †

After the ground has been " marked off," " picketed," or "lined," (by so many different terms is this work designated) the next work to be entered upon is " Holing," or " Pitting," one far more arduous and costly. This consists in making a hole of from 1½ to 2 feet wide and deep, in every spot where a picket stands, in which the plant is to be placed.

No pit should be less than 18 inches deep, though in loose, rich soils, so much depth is not required, as in those which are stiff and dry ; one of the objects of a deep pit is to enable the roots of the plant to descend to such a depth, as may be necessary for it to obtain moisture from the

---

* Loudon.
† Abridged Coffee Planter of St. Domingo.

ground in the dry weather. Thus there are some situations where the soil is so free as to permit the tap-root to penetrate to sufficient depth without any previous excavation, though it is not safe to rely on this being so in any case.

As a general rule, the deeper and wider the pit made, the better chance the plant has of a quick growth : some persons, however, suppose that if the pit be very deep, in windy situations, the tap-root will be unable to penetrate to the undisturbed soil, and that, consequently, the plant will not have sufficiently firm hold in the ground.

The usual sized pit is eighteen inches cube; of these an ordinary coolie will, in commonly loose soil, make from 20 to 30, though in some localities, where the ground is excessively hard or gravelly, they will be unable to make more than about 18 in a day.

In making 25 holes at 18 inches cube, 1,45,800 inches is removed, this is only equal to about 10½ 2-feet pits, though a coolie can make from 16 to 20 2-feet pits at the same rate ; this may be accounted for by the fact that it is more easy to excavate in a wide than in a narrow space.

In undertaking pitting, it should always be recollected that a narrow pit may at any time be remedied by subsequent trenching, &c., a shallow one never, and it is, therefore, better to be on the safe side : frequently also a stone may lie under the pit at a depth of only a few inches, this will generally cause the death of the plant in the dry weather.

It will be seen that this is a tedious and arduous work, as well as a most important one, and, indeed, it is the slowest of all works undertaken in coffee cultivation.

This is a fact worthy of remembrance, in order that the planter may not fell more land than he will be able to pit in the right season. It should be commenced in January or February, or as soon as possible after the land is cleared, and may be continued 5 or 6 months.

Contracts for this work are occasionally given, the rates varying between £1 and Rupees 18 per 1,000.

For this work a coolie should be provided, with a mammotie and a crowbar or digger: the spade end of the latter is useful in digging down the sides and bottom of the pit, while the pointed one is used to pick out stones.

Pits should not be made too deep where the subsoil is clayey, as in this case they will prove receptacles for water, and the root of the plant will become rotted.

After the pits have been left open for a certain time, (in order to permit their surface to be well aired,) they should be "filled in." This should be done by having the *surface soil* all round dug into them, avoiding the red gravelly earth, which will probably have been removed from the pit's bottom; care must be taken not to put in stones, or roots, weeds, &c., as the latter are apt to foster grubs, which will eventually attack the roots of the plant.

"Filling in" should be undertaken in wet weather or when the ground is moist, so that the sides of the pits should not be hard or caked, as in this case the roots of the plant will have difficulty in penetrating beyond its limits.

Women and boys can do this work very well, and from 60 to 70 pits a day carefully filled is fair work for them.

If the pits be on the side of a steep hill, only the ground

on the upper sides should be dug into them, the lower side being carefully preserved as a retaining wall.

If left to themselves, coolies in filling the pits are apt simply to shovel in the earth which has been previously taken out, this is a great mistake for several reasons, and should never be permitted ; by digging in the sides of the pits from the surface, an increased area of loosened soil is given to the tender roots of the young plant, and the surface mould consisting of the decayed organic matter is supplied for its nourishment.

Besides these objects, it should be recollected that a pit left open for any length of time is apt in most soils to get crusted inside, in which case it operates much in the same way as a flower-pot, and by cutting in the sides, a great portion of this crust will be destroyed.

CHAPTER X.

PLANTING.

PLANTING is the most important work of all, and should be the most carefully executed, as, on its success, depend the prospects of the estate. The manner in which plants are put in must be determined by the size and age of those used. " Stumps"* are the hardiest and safest, more especially in uncertain weather, and strike readily, where the ground has become saturated with moisture. Before planting, their roots should be carefully pruned and trimmed with the knife, and the stump cut to the proper length above the roots, which is six inches.

The object of pruning the roots is, that the ends which have been injured in removing the plant from its original position, may be cut fairly and clearly off, and that no root may be left of sufficient length to render it liable to be doubled or twisted in the planting : the tap-root should be about 9 inches long, and the laterals about 4 inches ; if two tap-roots be growing together on one plant, one should be cut off.

---

* It has been observed, however, that " Stumps" cannot be used with success in districts where a long dry season immediately succeeds the monsoon ; as in Wynaad.

It is important, in pruning the roots, to observe that they be cut clean through with a sharp knife, and not broken or torn.

If small nursery plants be selected for use, these require much more delicate handling : in taking them out of the nursery, a rainy, dark day should be chosen ; the earth should be gently prised up with a crowbar, all round, and each plant carefully removed, with as much earth as will adhere to the roots. This earth should then be pressed gently round the roots between the hands, the plants placed in baskets, and carried off for distribution, one being laid down at each pit.

In very wet climates, where a continuance of uninterrupted rainy weather may with certainty be calculated upon, all this care in removing the plants " with ball" as it is termed, is unnecessary, but in any case no plant should be kept out of the ground *a moment longer than is absolutely necessary.*

In putting in the plants it should be carefully observed that the roots are straightly laid out, and that neither tap-root or feeders are doubled up.

The best method of performing the operation of planting is as follows : a boy or girl having laid down at the pit the plant intended for it, a man provided with a mammotie follows ; he then strikes the blade of the mammotie deeply into the pit in order to loosen and break up the mould, then chops it up. A stroke is then given with the mammotie as deep as it will go into the centre of the pit : the handle is then drawn towards the labourer, while its blade remains in the ground : by this means a vacuity is formed between the back of the mammotie and the ground, into which the coolie with his other hand introduces the roots of the plant, being careful to put them to the bottom of the opening, he then takes out the mammotie gently, so as not to displace or disarrange them, lays it aside and presses in the earth with his now disengaged right hand. The plant should then be drawn gently upwards, to make sure that the roots are unbent; after which the earth may be firmly trodden down (if in light soil) until the latter retains no longer the impression of the foot.*

The operation termed " puddling," is performed by mixing a quantity of stiff earth or clay with water, to the consistency of gruel, and dipping the roots, or the whole of the "Stump" in it; in this manner the natural moisture is retained, as well as an additional supply attracted : with reference to " puddling," Mr. Loudon remarks : " When the plants have been brought from a distance, he (Pontey) strongly recommends *puddling* them previously to planting ; if they seem very much dried, it would be still better to lay them in the ground for 8 or 10 days, giving them a good soaking of water every second or third day, in order to restore their vegetable powers ; for it well deserves notice, that a degree

---

* " On very steep slopes which have been pitted, the following rules ought to be observed in planting ; to place the plant in the angle formed by the declivity and surface of the pit ; and in finishing, to raise the lower margin of the pit, whereby the plant will be made to stand as if on level ground, and the moisture be retained in the hollow of the angle, evidently to its advantage." " Green, or unpractised hands are apt to double the roots, * * * a careful man, however, will become, if not a speedy, at least a good planter, in one day, and it is of more importance that he be a sure hand, than a quick one."—*Planting Calendar*, " *Loudon*."

of moisture in soil, sufficient to support a plant recently or immediately taken from the nursery, would, in the case of dried ones, prove so far insufficient, that most of them would die in it."

There is some diversity of opinion as to the size and age of plants which ought to be selected for planting out; it is not, however, a question which can be decided by any fixed rules, but must, in a great measure, be regulated by the climate of the locality for which they are required. In Ceylon, where the planting season is frequently interrupted by bursts of sunshine, the use of nursery plants, permitted to retain their leaves, is precarious, unless taken up with a ball of earth round their roots, which is a slow and tedious operation: the result is that Ceylon planters usually prefer " stumps." These latter are to be recommended for several reasons; they can be kept much longer out of the ground than plants, and are not affected by sunshine immediately after planting, *provided the ground be wet.* Under favorable circumstances, they will throw out a number of sprouts within a month or five weeks after planting: in three months the strongest of these should be selected, and the remainder broken off.

Where dull rainy weather can be depended on, nursery *plants* of the second year are most satisfactory, as, if quickly put in, they will appear hardly to have ceased growing at all in the transplanting; but, if before they have struck root, an hour or two sunshine should intervene, they will immediately droop, cast all their leaves which are full grown, and many of them probably die.

Nursery *plants* of the first season are very unsafe when

they have subsequently to withstand a long dry season, as the roots will not have got sufficiently below the surface to enable them to gain moisture; they are, moreover, easily choked up and killed by weeds, which unfortunately, cannot always be kept down, especially at low elevations, in Bamboo or chena lands.

If plants of the third year are to be used, as thick in the stem as the little finger, I should recommend stumping them down in the nursery in January; they will then throw out sprouts, or suckers, which will be nine inches long by June; they may then be planted out and two good shoots (those nearest the root being the best) selected. These should be allowed to grow together for a month, after which one should be broken off and the other left. I have seen this course answer better than either plants or simple stumps.

It is worthy of attention, that coolies in planting with a stake, or a crowbar, are apt to "hang" the plants, namely, to press the earth round the throat of the plant only, while a vacuity is left round the roots: indeed, where the soil is stiff or in lumps, and a deep narrow hole is made with a crowbar for the plant, this can hardly be avoided. The result is, that for a few weeks the plant will bear a healthy appearance, but on the advent of fine weather will immediately die. For this reason, *narrow, pointed implements* should never be used for planting.

In Europe, in making plantations, an instrument named, the "diamond dibber" is used for this purpose, and, doubtless, it might be introduced with advantage on coffee estates. It is thus described, as applied to dibbling: this "is the cheapest and most expeditious planting of any we yet know. * * * The plate of the dibber is made of good steel, and is four inches and a half broad where the iron handle is welded to it; each of the other two sides of the triangle is 5 inches long; the thickness of the plate one-fifth part of an inch, made thinner from the middle to the sides, till the edges become sharp. The length of the iron handle is seven inches, and sufficiently strong not to bend working, or six-eighths of an inch square; the iron handle is furnished with a turned hilt, like the handle of a large gimlet, both in its form and the manner of being fixed on." In planting with this instrument, it may be used in the same manner, as described above with reference to the mammotie.

It will be evident that if pitting could be dispensed with, an estate could be formed at a less expense and with much more facility: this has often been tried, and the plants simply "dibbled in," which method has, in some cases, answered tolerably well. The objects of pitting are simply to give free scope to the roots of the coffee, in pulverized soil, while young and tender, and to prevent their being interfered with by the original forest roots or by stones: now, should these evils not exist, *i. e.*, should the surface soil be deep and free, and not bound together by roots, and should there be no stones or gravelly substratum, to obstruct the tap-root of the plants, pitting will not be necessary. Unfortunately, however, a soil of such a conformation as this, rarely, if ever, presents itself to the planter.

In bamboo land, where a dense scrub jungle will spring up within a few months after clearing, and the ground be rendered invisible by a luxuriant crop of fine grass, it will be evident that the surface soil must be comparatively matted with roots, and that "pitting," therefore, cannot be dispensed with; and even in forest land, where the roots are principally those of felled trees, and where after a good burn, the blackened surface will remain clear of vegetation for a long period, still dibbling is not advisable, on the same grounds, as may be proved by digging a pick into the ground, where a mass of roots will be found broken and turned up by the operation.

Dibbling should never, therefore, be adopted, except in land possessing a deep, friable soil, and where, at an early subsequent period, it will be practicable to dig up the soil in the neighbourhood of each plant.

In any case, dibbling with the crowbar is a very objectionable method, as the hole formed by it being simply caused by compression, the ground at the sides is rendered hard and impervious.

The best mode appears to me to be what is in Scotland called the "slit" method of planting, and might be performed by an instrument, made like the shingle splitter, described in another chapter, only having a longer handle, say 4 feet; or by a digger with a crowbar having a very long, broad, and sharp spade-end; this would answer the same purpose as a spade, only being handled differently.

"The operator with his spade makes three cuts 12 or 15 inches long, crossing each other in the centre, at an angle of 60 degrees, the whole having the form of a star, he inserts the spade across one of the rays a few inches from the centre, and on the side next himself; then bending the handle towards himself and almost to the ground, the earth opening in fissures from the centre, in the direction of the cuts which had been made, he, at the same time, inserts his plant at the point where the spade intersected the ray, pushing it forward to the centre, and assisting the roots in rambling through the fissures. He then lets down the earth by removing his spade," and it is then trampled down.

In "dibbling," the lateral roots of the plant should be pruned closer to the main root, than when planting in pits.

CHAPTER XI.

Resumé.

ROADS—DRAINING.

In the preceding chapters I have endeavoured to dispose of all the primary operations in the *formation* of a coffee estate, I will now proceed to describe the various processes necessary for its proper up-keep and cultivation, in the order and season in which they come round

The proper season for commencing to fell, build coolie lines, and make the nursery, is October or early in November; these works should be all completed by the middle of January.

The land should be burned off early in February, and cleared up *at once*.

Immediately after clearing, "line" and picket the land : trace out the roads ; and then commence pitting, which may be continued till the middle of June, in which season the plants may be put in ; June, July, and the early part of August being the wet monsoon months, they are the most suitable time of year for planting, though in Ceylon, owing to a difference of season from Southern India, it is usually done earlier.

The land having been all planted, it should be carefully weeded once a month, by hand if possible.

After the first weeding, or if performed by women and children, while it is going on, the men may be employed in opening up the roads which had been traced after "lining" probably in March; and also in making catch-drains in order to preserve the soil from washing away.

About six weeks or two months after the first planting, go through the land again, and remove all the stumps or plants which have died or are not looking well, and supply their places with good healthy plants, if the *planting weather* still continues.

Having proceeded thus far without mentioning the making of roads in any previous chapter, it might be supposed that I had overlooked the subject, but this is by no means the case; but though the roads *should all be traced* as soon as the land has been cleared and lined, I am of opinion that the *cutting* of them should be left over till it has been planted up. Planting operations, owing to the cessation of rain, *must* be stopped at a certain date, and it is much better that the planter should have as much time as possible to devote to them within that date, deferring a work of this kind to a more convenient season.

Good and well traced roads are most important features on an estate, they not only add to the facility of working it, and give it a tasteful appearance, but are also useful in *stopping the wash* on the hill slopes, caused by the rain.

A good "Bandy-road" will subsequently be a valuable adjunct to the estate, and a trace suitable for one at as easy a gradient as possible, not steeper than 1 in 15, should be marked out; this road should go right through the centre of the estate, passing the spot intended for "*the works*," and come out at such a place, that a connection between it and the nearest public cart-road, may be easily effected: as its principal uses will be for the transport of crop and manure, (for neither of which purposes it will be required for the first two years,) it need not at first be made more than six feet wide, unless labour is plentiful.

Several other roads, running to all parts of the plantation, should be cut, all converging to the store, where the coolies are mustered and the crop eventually brought in. There should be at least two roads to the bungalow, one from the entrance of the estate, and one from the store.

When the coolies are picking crop, they place their large bags of coffee on the road, filling them from the small bags they have tied round their waists, hence the length of a line of coffee between two roads should not be too great, or much delay will be caused them in passing to and fro: I should therefore say, that on a hill side the parallel paths should not generally be more than 100 or 150 yards apart. This may appear a lavish use of the land, but I do consider that there is any waste, as the coffee trees immediately below a road are always finer and more productive than the others, owing, doubtless, to the earth thus thrown round their roots.

All these roads, or bridle paths, should be marked out with a road tracer, at an easy gradient, and with an eye to taste and effect as well as utility. An excellent instrument is sold by the machinery-makers in Kandy; it consists of a brass tube hung on the side of a pole, this tube must be the height of the eye; below it is a graduated scale, with the gradients from 1 in 5, to 1 in 20, for ascent and descent, marked on it with notches; from this scale depends a weight, by shifting which to any notch such an inclination is given to the tube as the gradient of the road is intended to have. The end of the tube to which the eye is to be applied has a small hole bored in it, the other end a larger orifice, across which a horizontal line of wire is placed; the person about to trace, holds the instrument now described, having affixed the gradient; a coolie then proceeds some 10 or 15 yards in front of him, holding a cross of exactly the same height as the tube, the coolie is then directed to move up or down on the face of the hill till the centre of the cross is bisected by the horizontal wire in the furthest end of the telescope.

A picket is then placed on the spot discovered, the coolie moves on 10 yards or so further, and the tracer is brought and placed at this spot, another sight taken, and so on.

Another coolie should now follow with small pegs 6 inches long, and plant one in the ground close to the first picket, hammering it in till its head only is visible; by cutting the ground above this peg down to its level, and by throwing the earth excavated, on the lower side or *outside it*, the true level will be gained.

In making a road through a clearing, a gang of men with axes and cross-cut saws, should be one day's work in advance of the next party, who should be provided with levers to roll off all the logs which have been cut through; another working party should follow with mamooties, pick-axes and crowbars, and complete the work.

Performed by Estate coolies or by contract, a road four feet in the solid should cost about £10 or £12 per mile, exclusive, of coure, of blasting, or extensive building up.

In blasting rocks, many bad accidents frequently happen, through the inexperience of those who undertake it; it may be useful, therefore, and appropriate to this chapter, if I give a short account of the manner in which this operation may be safely and effectually performed. A substitute for it, when the mass of rock to be removed is not very great, may sometimes be obtained by making large fires on the rock till it is quite hot, and then suddenly dashing bucketsful of cold water on it, when it will generally split and crack in every direction.

For *Blasting*, there are several implements required, *i. e.*, jumpers for boring, and these are generally made octagonally of steel; some good hammers, and long spoons for removing the powdered stone.

Coolies are usually tasked to make 36 inches of bore in a day, though, unless practised at the work, they will not generally accomplish more than about 30 inches, in granite, or other hard rocks.

When the bores are complete, *clean them well* out with the spoon, and then with tow, observing that no grits be left in. When perfectly clean, the ramrod comes into use: this is made generally of iron, though it would be better of some metal, which would not strike fire, when brought in conjunction with stone;* along one side of this, a groove is inscribed, in which the fusee may lie when the loading is going on.

With the ramrod first push down into the bottom of the bore a ball of *clean dry tow* or torn *gunny:* next put in

---

* *Gun metal* would, I believe, answer the purpose.

the charge of powder, in the proportion of 1 *inch of powder* to 6 *inches or* 8 *inches* of *bore*. Next take fusee, and, cutting it to a length of about (6) *six inches or more than the depth of the bore*, open out with the fingers one end of it for about a quarter of an inch, so that the powder which it contains may be made to come in contact with the loading, then *straighten it* and put it down along one side of the bore *till the end goes well into the charge.* Next *put down a wad of tow* or torn gunny *over the charge.* Now take *some sand-stone*, and break it up, into small pieces, the size of the little finger nail, or of *good-sized peas, and sprinkle* this *with water till quite moist;* put in a small quantity (about a tea spoonful at a time,) and knock it down with the ramrod, *gently* at first, but till it is quite firm and close, then put in more, and hammer the ramrod down on it till it also has become a part of the first, and so on, increasing in the strength of the hammering, till the bore is completely filled.

Now remove all implements, coats, &c., from the vicinity of the rock; open out the end of the fusee, which protrudes some 6 inches from the bore, lay in the opened part a few grains of gunpowder, *apply a fire stick*, and GET OUT OF DANGER!!

DRAINING.

Nearly all coffee estates, lying more or less on hill slopes, the soil during the heavy rains of the monsoon is extremely liable to wash, and, to prevent this, recourse must be had to trenches or drains across the face of the hill: the more frequently these occur, *the better*, and they will not only prevent any of the soil from being lost, but will do it a great deal of good, by lightening and sweetening it. If the trenches are made quite close together, they may be very nearly level, but in any case they should have slight tendency to descend, in order to prevent their filling or bursting; if at an easy gradient, the soil will be effectualy retained in them, and the water may be made to run off to the next ravine, or nullah.

The fewer the trenches are, the greater will be the amount of water and earth which will accumulate in them.

The gradient should never be greater than 1 in 12, and the trenches should be 15 to 18 inches wide, and at least one foot deep on the lower side. A few hands should always be sent round after a heavy fall of rain to empty them with the mamootie.

On this subject, Mr. Wall, of Ceylon, says, :—" I have no hesitation in saying that surface draining is the most profitable operation in coffee cultivation. It not only directly accomplishes a most important object in preventing the washing away of soil by heavy rains, but it also prepares the way for modes of cultivation which would otherwise become impracticable.

" It is surprising to see the indifference with which planters witness the loss of thousands of tons of their best soil, by the wash of heavy rains; and whilst they use their most strenuous efforts to improve their soil, they scarcely do anything to prevent its being carried away. True economy suggests that whatever we may do to improve it, we ought at least to preserve the soil we have. Draining, systematically and judiciously carried out, is an effectual preventive of wash."

In swampy or sour soils, coffee should never be planted, as, unless thoroughly drained, the plants will die from the perspiration at the roots being checked, and their subsequent rotting. Draining swampy ground is an expensive and labourious operation, and should never be resorted to when land is abundant and labour scarce.

Swampy grounds may be turned to great advantage, by planting on them a succulent juicy description of grass, termed " Mauritius grass ;" this is an excellent fodder for the cattle kept for manuring purposes, and grows most luxuriantly in swamps, which would otherwise be entirely useless. Mauritius grass is most easily propagated, it is a creeping grass and throws out root fibre from each joint which touches the ground. Under these circumstances, it has to be used with some caution, as, when taken out of the manure pit with the manure and applied to the coffee, it is apt to spring up in every direction, and is then very difficult to eradicate ; the only method being to put it into bags and carry it off to a distance, when weeding.

To obviate this evil, a grass-cutting machine should be used ; this can be worked by two men, or be connected by a belt with the water wheel ; the grass will then be chopped up into small bits, of about an inch in length, and be less liable to take root.

CHAPTER XII.

WEEDING, FILLING UP VACANCIES.

WEEDING is a most important and indispensable work and must be early attended to, for several reasons. Cultivated plants should have the full benefit of the soil on which they are placed. Weeds have an exhaustive effect on the soil, smother objects of cultivation, and absorb quantities of moisture: being of more rapid and frequent growth than coffee, they rob the latter of that nourishment and moisture which it only should receive; they also deprive the soil of that atmospheric moisture, which it would otherwise have absorbed. Another deleterious effect which weeds, especially of the grass description, have on the ground, is, that their roots bind the soil so closely that it cannot easily be penetrated by the atmospheric influences, nor by the roots of the plants.

It should be remembered that in a coffee estate every shrub, plant or herb, not expressly intended for growth, *is a weed*.

The means of removing weeds are, by pulling them out by the hand, hoeing them up, or by using the hand-scraper; and of destroying them, by exposing them to the sun and air, burying, or burning them.

In commencing to weed early, much subsequent loss will be avoided, and the work should be systematically pursued once a month, *or oftener, if necessary:* unfortunately, however, this is not generally practicable, owing to scarcity of labour, and hence many estates are frequently seen in a deplorable condition in this respect.

Of the methods of removing weeds above named, each has its advantages and drawbacks under different circumstances and in different localities.

Weeding by hand, should be practised on all steep slopes, where it is not desirable to stir the surface soil, lest it should be washed off; and where the weed not being abundant, the operation will not be too slow : on new forest-clearings where the soil is not naturally sown with grass, and other low tenacious weeds, producing only sow thistle, goat-weeds and other tall plants, weeding in this manner is easily performed : each weeder should be provided with a small sack, tied round the waist, into which he can thrust all that are in flower or seed ; the bags can be emptied into pits made for the purpose at convenient distances in the land ; or on the road, in which case they be subsequently burned or buried at pleasure.

With the scraper, weeding is practised on steep slopes when it is desirable to disturb the surface as little as possible, but where the growth is too low, minute and numerous, for eradication by the hand. From being much lighter and smaller, the scraper penetrates less into the soil than the mamootie. Scrapers made in Ceylon for this purpose, consist of a piece of hoop iron, about fifteen inches in length, bent round at one end and pointed at the other. A common piece of hoop iron off a barrel, bent into a curve near one end answers equally well.

With the mamootie. On flat level fields, where no wash is to be apprehended, hoeing freely and deeply is the best mode of weeding, as by this method the soil is also pulverized, and the sun and air admitted into it. Digging up the soil tends more than anything else to improve its quality, and is, in fact, nearly as important as weeding itself ; it allows free scope to the roots ; and also enables the soil to absorb moisture, by increasing its capillary attraction or sponge-like capability ; stiff, clayey soil particularly require frequent digging up, as, without it, they either do not absorb moisture at all, or, having at last absorbed it, are too retentive.

" *Burying in.*" This is another and an effectual plan, where the weeds are high and rank : in doing this, a wide shallow hole is dug, and all the weeds for several feet round are dug into it, and the pit covered over.

On estates in Ceylon, contracts are usually given to Canganies to weed, at so much per acre per month. In these, the contractor has to provide and pay his own coolies, and to weed the portion allotted to him, once a month. Contract weeding is an excellent system, and should every where be adopted where practicable : on clean estates the price varies from 1s. to 2s. an acre ; but on old estates which have at one time been weedy, and consequently contain seed, 2s. 6d. to 4s. per acre monthly. By this arrangement, large estates may be regularly weeded cheaply and without anxiety or supervision.

Filling up Vacancies.

In all newly planted clearings, as well as old fields of coffee, many plants occasionally die off, leaving a gap; these vacancies should be systematically filled up. Plants are killed from many different causes; young plants frequently die from having been put in with the roots bent; from a flat stone at the bottom of the pit obstructing the advance of the tap-root, from being smothered with weeds; and from drought or else swampiness.

Old trees are more liable to attacks from insects and grubs, and hence numbers die from the entrance of worms or grubs into the roots or stem; from consumption; from dropsy; or from other diseases incident to all classes of plants.

As prevention is better than cure, it will be well to avoid these dangers, which can, in the case of young plants, be done at the outset, by careful planting, good pitting, and keeping them free of weeds: for old trees, pulverizing the soil, careful pruning and sufficient manuring.

However, notwithstanding every precaution and care, a number of plants will die, and their places must be filled up in the following manner. The original pit must be re-emptied, *and enlarged an inch or two in width and depth*, particularly the latter; this should be done in the dry weather and the pit left open for some time, being only filled when it is necessary to plant.

In old soils, or when the vacancy is surrounded by old trees, it will be necessary to make a large pit, in order that the new plant may not be incommoded by the roots of the old trees : and, indeed, it will be better to make a ring trench round it for this purpose if practicable, a foot deep and a few inches wide will be sufficient to isolate the plant. It will also sometimes be necessary to put a basketful of new soil into each pit near the surface ; or should the soil be much exhausted, a few handsful of Poonac, pounded and mixed with the soil, will be of benefit : should poonac not be procurable, a little rotten dung or compost will suffice.

It will be quite futile to go to the labor and expense of filling up vacancies, unless the ground round the new plants be kept subsequently perfectly free of weeds.

CHAPTER XIII.

SHELTER, PROTECTION, AND SHADE.

Staking is a work undertaken to protect the plants from the effects of the wind; in exposed situations the sooner this is done the better, though it is not required until the plants are, at any rate, 10 or 12 inches in height.

For small plants in the first season, the lining picket may be used for this purpose; but for larger plants a good stout stake 3 to $3\frac{1}{2}$ feet long, of sufficient strength not to bend, and well pointed, so as to penetrate easily into the ground, should be used.

Should any particular direction of wind prevail, this should be observed. The stake should enter the ground about 6 inches from the plant, at such a slant that it will touch the latter at about half its height from the ground, on the *windward side*. Should the stake be inserted among the young roots, it will do much injury to them, and if to the leeward of the plant, the latter will chafe much, get its branches broken, and its bark rubbed off.

The stake must be firmly knocked into the ground with a mallet, so as to form an efficient and steady support. The plant should be connected with the stake by a broad band of jungle or other fibre in an open loop, or figure of eight, of which the stem of the plant occupies one opening and the stake the other: the string must not be tied round the stem, as, if this is done, the plant gradually increasing in size, the bark will grow over the fastening, as I have often seen to happen. Should the stakes be of good wood not liable to decay, they will last two or three years, by which time the plants will generally have obtained so firm a hold in the ground as to require no artificial support.

For fastenings, strips of aloe leaf, the inner bark of many descriptions of trees, jungle rope, or coir yarn, may be used. Should the plant, before, or notwithstanding the precaution of staking, have got worked round in the ground, the best remedy is, besides the insertion of a stake, to earth it up some 5 or 6 inches from the ground.

Some planters have a belt of jungle to protect their coffee from the wind; but the opinions as to the advantage of this course differ, some persons stating that belts cause the wind to form itself into eddies or whirlwinds, and thus to do more injury than if permitted free course.

The European method in making plantations is to plant some quick growing shrub in rows to protect the young plants. Others plant hedges. I recollect a gentleman in Ceylon erecting a wall some 8 or 10 feet high of posts and brushwood, along the most exposed part of his estate with much benefit; these, however, are all expensive operations, and staking combined with low topping ought to be sufficient protection in moderately sheltered situations, and an exposed one, as I said before, ought not to be planted with coffee.

In hot, dry situations, where seasons of drought are frequent and prolonged, experience has shewn that coffee requires protection from the sun as well as the wind : the only practicable method of doing this, is by leaving them when felling, or subsequently planting trees, for shade.

It is a well known fact that some trees act as a blight on coffee, if growing near it, while the proximity of others has a beneficial effect : as this is a subject not generally understood, I will try and throw a little light upon it. It is, I believe, not generally known, though no less a fact, that plants give out an excrement from their roots perhaps analogous to the same process in the animal kingdom ; this would, perhaps, account for the injurious effect of the vicinity of some trees to coffee, as an excrement beneficial as manure, to one description of plant, might probably be noxious to others of a different species.

Again, many trees, instead of delving down into the subsoil for their sustenance, their roots are apt to spread about the surface, thus interfering with the nourishment and moisture, the full benefit of which ought to be exclusively devoted to the coffee.

Thirdly, every naturalist will be aware, that many trees exhale noxious gases, which render the atmosphere deleterious to other vegetation : this is especially found to be the case in Europe with regard to the elder, walnut, and laburnum trees.

On the other hand, besides their shade, many trees have other beneficial influences which ought to be considered ; the cover given to the ground causes the vegetable matter in the surface soil to decay more rapidly, and thus renders it more permeable to the fibres of the coffee roots ; then the continual falling of dead leaves adds to the soil the best description of enriching matter in large quantities, and as these are formed from nourishment principally extracted from the sub-soil, they add to the surface, for the benefit of the coffee, matter which the latter would otherwise never have reached; besides these, the value of estates growing large quantities of useful timber is gradually permanently increasing: the time will arrive when all kinds of timber will, in Ceylon and Southern India, be worth ten times its present intrinsic value, whether as for fuel, building, or cabinet-making.

The jack is the best tree for planting on coffee estates, both as regards the value of its timber, and the benefit its shade affords the coffee, in hot, dry climates, which climates are those which produce it in the greatest perfection. This tree, the *Artocarpus integrifolia*, grows to a large size, it resembles and belongs to the same family as the Bread-fruit tree, it possesses an excellent timber, which is extensively used for building, making furniture, &c., being susceptible of a high polish, and having a pretty grain. The jack fruit weighs from 20 to 30 lbs., and is wholesome, though course and somewhat unpleasant in smell and flavour; it contains 200 to 300 seeds, each as big as a date; these are farinaceous, and pleasant as food when boiled or roasted. The cultivation of this tree is worthy of attention, and I cannot name any other which will answer the purposes of shade for coffee, equally well.

In Wynaad and elsewhere, many estates have the road-sides planted with the loquat tree. Coffee appears to thrive well under it, but I am not aware that the wood is of any value, in which case it cannot be placed in comparison with the jack. The loquat is a pleasant fruit, yellow, and the size of a plum when ripe.

Trees when planted for shade should not be too close together, as they would then prevent a free circulation of air, which is necessary for coolness, and health of the coffee : the disposition of them should be irregular or quincunx, and the distance some 20 yards.

One of the most heavily bearing estates per acre in Ceylon, notwithstanding that in many parts of it the coffee trees stand 8 feet apart, is thickly studded with jack trees, without which indeed the sun would have burnt it up years ago.

With a view to make the trees throw out large leafy heads, and increase the extent of ground covered, the trees should be pruned to single stems, for 10 or 12 feet from the ground, this will also tend to produce large, straight, and valuable timber; moreover, the rays of the morning and evening sun which are mild and beneficial, will not then be excluded.

When travelling last year, I met an old French gentleman, who informed me that in the Mauritius the coffee and sugar planters use, for the purpose of shade, a very quick growing plant; unfortunately I cannot ascertain its name, but this gentleman gave as his opinion that by planting this shrub thickly with the coffee, the latter might be cultivated with success in the plains. The most rapid growing plant I am acquainted with, which would be of any use, is the castor-oil plant (Ricinus communis or Palma christi), it will grow from 6 to 10 feet in a year, and bears a crop of the seeds from which the oil is expressed in the first season. Its cultivation will require no trouble or care, but it will take a great deal of moisture from the surface soil, and neither can it be much recommended as a shade-yielding plant, as its foliage is not very luxuriant.

Plantains and bananas were evidently invariably planted for shade in St. Domingo, and I am quite sure, from personal observation, that these will do but little harm in any way to the coffee if planted in it, probably they might be useful, and do good.

CHAPTER XIV.

BUNGALOWS AND LINES.

Comfortable, permanent, and well-formed buildings will not only greatly add to the value of an estate, but contribute to the health and contentedness of the persons who reside on it; when, therefore, all the more immediately necessary works in the formation of a young estate have been completed, and a slackness of work succeeds for a time before the coffee comes into "full bearing," a bungalow for the Manager, and lines for the coolies, of a substantial and "pukka" character, should be erected.

"Pukka" buildings are also really more economical than temporary ones, which require that endless repair and renovation which run away with so much labour and money year by year.

I have seen given as the proper definition of a bungalow, a substantial, verandahed, one-storied place of residence: such a building may be built of various material, and in many different styles, and as its erection is an expensive and laborious undertaking, the subject should receive considerable previous attention.

Of the different materials of which the walls may be

made, I may mention the following, namely, stone and mortar, bricks and mortar, bricks or stone and mud: bricks may be either sun-dried or burnt, if the former process only is resorted to they will readily crumble away if at all subjected to the influence of damp or wet—wattle and mud, and, lastly, wooden boards.

The strongest houses are undoubtedly those which are composed of stone and mortar, but they are also the most expensive and tedious of erection, involving generally immense outlay in coolie labor for collecting and carrying the stones, of which a much greater quantity are required than would be the case in other materials, for the reason that walls of undressed stone should not be less than one foot and a half thick. In stone-walls, all the door-ways and windows should be arched; the arches may be made of bricks, if such are procurable. The expense of erecting a bungalow of these materials can only be determined or estimated by a knowledge of the distance at which suitable stone is found, and the means which are available for its conveyance to the required spot.

Bricks, in my opinion, form the most preferable material for house building : they are cheap, strong, easily carried and built, and may be made from almost any soil ; a common mason will lay from 4 to 500 large sized bricks each weighing 7 lbs. : of which, a coolie will carry 8 ; bricks of this weight will be about $10\frac{1}{2} \times 5\frac{1}{4} \times 3\frac{1}{2}$ inches in size.

The tests of good bricks, are their freedom from cracks, their hardness, and uniformity of size, also their giving out a ringing sound when struck, and their not much increasing in weight by immersion in water.

An useful pamphlet on this subject, applicable to the Madras Presidency, has afforded me some of the useful hints on brick-making which I give below.

The best size is, length $8\frac{3}{4}$ inches, breadth $4\frac{1}{4}$, and depth 2, each brick with the mortar quarter inch joint, will then occupy $9 \times 4\frac{1}{2} \times 2\frac{1}{4}$ inches.

Thicker bricks would be better, if they could be equally well burned, both as regards the smaller number required, and their smaller liability to be broken, in carrying from the works to the kiln.

The best brick earth consists of a mixture of pure clay and sand, free from stones; five parts of clay, to one of sand being the best proportion : earth of this quality and of these proportions, will often be found in its natural state ; but bricks may be made of almost any description of earth, provided it is free from pebbles and is not too sandy.

It is a good plan to break up the soil intended for brick-making, some months before its being used, as by this means it mellows. The tempering is usually performed by men treading the clay mixed with water under their feet, but the treading may be better done by buffaloes or any other cattle, or by elephants.*

The piece of ground, the soil of which it is intended to use, having been well cleared, it is dug up to the depth of a foot, and as much water as possible turned in upon it over night : the next morning turn in the cattle and let them tramp through it for, at least, two hours ; then let in some more water, and leave the mud till next day, or if time is wanting and this cannot be done, then repeat the tramping

---

* As in Kandy.

at once, and continue it until the earth is in a homogeneous paste. Only use sufficient water to make the clay plastic for the moulder; the next operation is to level and smooth off a bit of ground adjacent, on which the bricks when moulded may be laid.

The moulds should be of wood, bound with iron, and in such a form as to admit of making two bricks at once; they should also be a little larger than the intended size of the bricks, in order to allow for the shrinking of the clay in the burning. The manner in which the mould is applied is as follows: first dip it in water, place it on the ground, and then dab in the wet clay: press this well in, smoothing the top with the wet hand, and remove any superfluous clay, then lift up the mould gently, and having removed it a few inches further on, repeat the process.

The bricks must now be thoroughly, but gradually dried, and with the latter view they should be protected from the sun and wind. When half dry, take them and scrape off any dirt that has adhered and lay them on *their sides.*

To *burn* the bricks, level a square piece of ground, lay down two layers of bricks in rows, with a space of one brick between each; in this space place firewood, and also above the bricks to the heighth of, say, six inches: next, place others diagonally in two layers as before, and again firewood six inches deep: now two courses of bricks on *edge,* above which place nine inches of firewood. The clamp may then be raised six or eight feet high, with one foot of firewood to every four layers of bricks. As the clamp is increasing in height, build a wall round it, of sufficient strength to prevent the bricks falling out as the wood is consumed. The bricks should not be packed too close together, and the fire should be lighted to windward, after which plaster up the top and sides with mud.

A large clamp of one lac of bricks would take a week to burn, but a smaller one a lesser period. After the fire has gone out, the bricks should be allowed to cool for a week before the clamp is opened.

For *Tile-making*, the clay should be prepared in the same manner as for bricks, if anything, *more* carefully tempered, and the earth required more clayey; they are moulded flat, and then bent over a semi-cylindrical piece of wood, off which they are gently slid on to the ground where they are left to dry.

Another method is as follows: the clay is dabbed unto the mould, which is previously sprinkled with brick dust or sand, the superfluous clay having been removed, the contents of the mould are pressed in and smoothed over with a flat piece of wood, and the newly made tile then placed on one previously ready made; it is then sprinkled with dust and the next placed on it, and so on, until a heap is collected. The heaps are left till next day and then re-bent and gently laid one by one on the ground to become thoroughly dry.

Tiles are burnt in a circular kiln, and must be carefully packed and slowly burned.

"*Wattle and Dab*" is a cheap, expeditious, and neat mode of building, which, if well done, will stand for a great number of years: the posts and lathes may be either of sawn timber, or be taken direct from the jungle; if of the former, the building will have a much better and more angular appearance. The posts should have a space of six inches between them, and the transverse lathes which are opposite to each other on both sides, the same. These lathes may be either tied or nailed to the posts, after which all the interstices and spaces filled up with well tempered mud, and a good-sized stone pushed into each square of mud.

After the first application of mud has thoroughly dried, another coating should be applied, covering all the wood work; when this is also dry, the wall may be properly plastered with mortar, and will then have quite as good an appearance as brick work.

I have seen bungalows of this description in localities abounding with white ants, which had nevertheless stood for upwards of 30 years.* And I account for the fact in the following manner—by a wonderful provision of nature white ants seldom eat away a post without leaving enough of it to ensure its stability, and they also deposit a sort of substitute for what they consume, probably with a view to preventing a destruction in which they themselves would be involved; hence, though walls of this kind, in tropical climates, lose most of the wood work in a course of years, they are not necessarily much weakened, as the mud work is sufficient to support itself on its own basis when hardened by time.

In Ceylon there are one or two descriptions of timber which are proof against the attacks of white ants; and in the Wynaad, blackwood, kino, and mutty, all of which kinds are abundant, have the same advantage.

Wooden houses have the disadvantage of being too combustible.

---

* Condesalle, near Kandy.

I was almost omitting to mention the most common material of which buildings in Ceylon and Southern India are erected on the Sea Coast, and in some other localities, namely, Laterite or Cabook. This is a peculiar sort of decomposed rock, or perhaps it may be most correctly described as a peculiar sort of clay, which becomes petrified by exposure.

It is excavated at about 6 to 10 feet below the surface, in bricks of about 15 × 9 × 6 inches in size, and when exposed to dry in the sun for a time, these bricks, though originally sufficiently soft to be cut with an axe or a trowel, become quite hard, and make good substantial walls which become firmer and stronger by age.

Roofs may be made of grass thatch, "cadjans," or the plaited leaves of the cocoanut tree, shingles, tiles, or iron sheets.

Thatch is generally the easiest attained on a Coffee estate, and as it affords the coolest roof, is the most commonly used: but its disadvantages are its great liability to combustion, and the necessity for putting on a fresh coat every year.

"*Cadjans*" make a very cool and water-tight roof, but are only procurable in localities where the cocoanut tree flourishes.

Shingles are strips of wood split into narrow boards of a certain length and nailed side by side much in the same manner as stated: they are, if made from good timber, a durable and water-tight covering. Any straight grained tree, not liable to rot, may be selected for making shingles, and the manner in which they are made is as follows:—A straight stem having been selected not more than 15 or 18 inches in diameter, it should be sawn into lengths of 22 inches: these should be split into such segments as will afford the greatest number of shingles, and this will be resolved by the judgment of the workman. Two men will be engaged in sawing off the blocks, two for splitting off the shingles, and two for *dressing* them. For splitting, an instrument shaped somewhat like a spade, or more correctly, like an enormous chisel, made entirely of iron, is required; the blade of this should be six inches square and the handle eighteen inches long, making two feet in all. The block being placed on its end, the splitter must be held by one man on the part of which it is desired to cause the split, while another man provided with a large mallet gives it a smart stroke.

Each shingle should be $\frac{1}{4}$ to $\frac{1}{2}$ of an inch in thickness, and from three to five inches in width.

After splitting, they are handed over to the other coolies to dress, or remove all roughnesses from the surfaces or edge. The shingles as prepared should be stacked in a shed, and if of green wood, left for six or eight months until their natural moisture has evaporated, as, unless cured in this manner, they will crack when exposed on the roof to the sun, especially after rain.

Six good men will prepare 600 shingles a day.

In putting them on the roof, some nicety and care is necessary: the first or bottom row should be double, and protruded some 4 or 6 inches beyond the end of the rafters. Each must be perforated carefully with a gimlet 3 inches from the upper end, and nailed on with a small $1\frac{1}{2}$ inch nail or sprig. If in boring or nailing the shingle should split, it should be discarded, unless either part so divided be of sufficient width to be used of itself, when a fresh puncture may be made.

A small space of one-third or half an inch should be left between each, to allow for expansion when wet. The lowest and first row having been put on *double*, that is, each of the upper shingles covering the space left between each of the lower ones, another row may be commenced, the end of each coming to within *seven inches* of the end of those beneath, and covering fifteen inches of the space between those beneath it. In this arrangement, it is calculated that of ordinary sized shingles, 6 or 7 will be required to cover the square foot.

The cost of cutting shingles is calculated, in Ceylon, at about 9 shillings per 1,000—putting on, from 3 to 4 shillings-nails, 4 shillings; thus, exclusive of carriage, a good covering for a house may be had at a comparatively small cost, which ought to require no renewal for from six to ten years.

Tiles require no description, they should only be used when the best clay is procurable, and when once on should not be removed oftener than once in two years, unless they let in water, when the part where the fault is should be repaired; they are a most lasting, in combustible roof, but are not as cool as thatch.

For *Roofing*, *Iron*, flat or corrugated, black or galvanized, is now-a-days extensively used in the erection of buildings for all purposes. In *coffee stores*, where heat and dryness are much required, they are excellent ; they are also valuable from their durability and safety from fire ; but for residences within the tropics they are quite unsuitable, rendering the heat within unbearable and making a great noise during wind and rain storms. A medical friend also assures me that iron roofing renders a bungalow unhealthy to live in from the great *variation* in the temperature it causes in the twenty-four hours, for whereas, during the heat of the day, it very much raises the temperature, in the night-time when the air is cold, it very much increases the latter condition of the atmosphere also.

Presenting a large surface, with but little weight, iron roofing sheets, and indeed entire roofs are frequently carried away by the wind : to obviate this danger, large stones or blocks of wood are generally laid over them. But even this is often insufficient, and I therefore insert the following letter from one of the oldest planters of Ceylon, to the Secretary of the Planter's Association, showing how such an extremely awkward contingency, as the sudden uncovering of a building, by the elements may be provided against :—

" Sir, when Colombus made the egg stand on end on the table, how simple the matter appeared to his audience. There is many an idea as simple but of far more utility. I had a store covered with corrugated iron, in an exposed situation ; if the sheets of this iron were fastened down at *both ends*, the simple principle of expansion and contraction of the iron, by the alternating degrees of heat and cold, very soon loosened the nails or rivets, and the sheets became loose. The manager of the estate became annoyed beyond endurance, by the blowing off by the wind of his store-roof, and in his desperation he screwed them to the rafters. The result was, that one blowy night the rafters and all were lifted off.

"John Gordon, the pulper maker, conceived the idea of rivetting slips of iron to one end of each sheet of iron, into which he slipped the end of the overlapping sheet, nailing the other end to the rafter, or reeper, and the other end being loose, slid up and down within the slip, according as the iron contracted or expanded, and thus he kept the iron firm and secure. Recently, on an emergency, I had to cover a store with iron. I could find none of Gordon's iron, but only plain sheets. In my dilemma, I mentioned the difficulty to a gentleman in Kandy, who tore off the cover of a Price Current, and shewed me how, by pieces of stiff hoop iron, bent in three to slip over the end of the upper sheet, and under that of the lower sheet, I might answer the purpose; so I procured these from Walker and Co., and nailed the upper end of the sheets to the rafters, and holding the lower ends of the next overlapping sheets, by means of these slips; the roof is all I could desire. The corrugation of the iron admits of expansion across the sheet, while the lateral expansion and contraction work up and down the hoop iron slips, and the nails are not loosened, nor the roof impaired.

"In gratitude to the friend who gave me the idea, I communicate the intelligence to my fellow-planters, through you, not doubting there may be some, who will be as thankful as I am, to know how to get over a difficulty, serious in itself, and in so very simple, inexpensive, and rational a manner.

Your's very truly,
(Signed) R. B. TYTLER,
Chairman.

November 1858.
The Secretary, Planters' Association.

The description of bungalow to be built, must, of course, depend on the amount of money which is to be devoted to its erection. In most localities, a commodious and suitable residence may be put up for between £300 and £400. Neither the requirements of the *Planter* will render necessary, nor his means allow, in most cases, the erection of a grand or expensive habitation, and it is neither prudent nor advisable to saddle the accounts of a young estate with a great outlay for an ornamental and superfluous style of architecture; comfort, neatness, stability, and *economy* are the only objects to be kept in view.

A bungalow which I built in 1855 in imitation of the Swiss Cottage style, raised 3 feet off the ground on stone pillars, with wooden floor, and weather-boarded walls, cost just about £100; it contained a sitting room, two bed-rooms and a verandah, and had a masonry fire-place in the centre room.

In houses raised off the ground, dryness and healthiness are attained, but the boards of the floor should be dove-tailed together, or the wind striking upwards through the interstices will render it too cold at night.

Bungalow *floors* may be made either of bricks, paving, tiles, plaster, asphalte, or wood. The best of all these is *Asphalte*, which is a mineral production resembling pitch, or perhaps more closely approaching in appearance to lava: it is poured on the floor boiling hot, having been mixed with a due proportion of sand while boiling; as it cools it is pressed and rubbed smooth, which, if well done, will cause it, when cold, to present the beautiful, hard, polished appearance of black marble. White ants cannot, if it be laid down carefully and of a proper thickness, make their way through it, a great advantage in localities where these destructive insects are numerous.

Chunam plaster, though neat, clean, and cool in appearance when new, soon gets broken up when much trampled upon, and is in that state most dirty and objectionable. *Dutch Tiles* for flooring are very durable and neat, but are very expensive and difficult of carriage; a good substitute for these may be made by using *common bricks*, joining them with mortar and " pointing" them.

Wooden floors require but little comment, they are so well known, but I may remark that the boards should be very narrow, say 5 or 6 inches wide by $1\frac{1}{2}$ inches thick; of this size, they will not be very liable to warp or curl, if well nailed down, nor will so small a width admit of decrease by shrinking.

Timber for sawing can generally be found in the clearing; if felled some time previously it will be cured and dried, and more suitable for use than green timber out of the forest.

In Ceylon, the rate paid to sawyers varies from 12s. to 14s. per 100 superficial feet, this includes cutting up and hoisting the log.

In Malabar, sawyers will neither fell, cut up, nor hoist their timber, this having to be accomplished by coolies, which often prevents planters from employing sawyers, owing to scarcity of hands. Under these circumstances, the rate charged on the coast at Calicut and Tellicherry is about Rs. 1-8 to Rs. 1-12 per candy; on the Hills, Rupees 2-12 to Rupees 3.

One candy is equal to 12 coles.

One cole is equal to 24 inches (Malayalum), or 28½ inches (English.)

The following is a simple manner of measuring sawyers' work in Ceylon, where the table is by feet and inches. Say a post 6 inches by 5 inches thick, by 21 feet in length, add 6×5 inches=11 inches. Multiply 21 by 11=231, now divide 231 inches by 12, the result=19 feet 3 inches. A board 9 inches wide, 1 inch thick, 24 feet long, multiply 9 by 24, divide by 12, the result is=18 feet.

In Malabar measurement, the method is different, the *cuts* of the saw are measured and not the size of the pieces sawn, and it may calculated as follows:—One log having been intersected by 6 cuts at 11 inches, by 5¼ coles; multiply 6 by 11 to produce 66, then multiply 66 by 5¼=346½, divide this by 24=14·10½, then divide this by 12, and the result of measurement is 1 candy, 2 coles, 10½ inches. Or say, 17 cuts @ 3½ inches by 5½ coles: multiply 17 by 3½=59½, multiply this by 5½=327¼, divide by 24, afterwards by 12, and the result will be = 1 candy, 1 cole, 15¼ inches.

In building COOLIE LINES, the planter should be most careful to select a healthy situation, sufficiently open, without being too much exposed to violent wind. The "landwind" of India is especially unhealthy, and comes laden with impurities and even diseases, from passing over large tracts of malarious and reeking country.

Water should be brought by a channel to the vicinity of the lines, and not, as is generally the case, the site of the lines, made to depend on the vicinity of a stream;

ravines and low grounds are always unhealthy, as the bad heavy gases float down off the higher and settle in them.

In line-building, ventilation is a great point to be attended to, and this object is best attained by the adoption of the following plan. Provide each set of lines with a verandah 6 or 7 feet wide, running along their entire length, making the verandah posts of the same height as the *back* wall; the *front* wall should not be built right up to the roof, but to within 1½ or 2 feet of it only, leaving open this space for the exit of foul air and smoke. Coolies prefer lines with a verandah, as this is useful for piling firewood, drying their wet cumblies in the monsoon, &c.

Cleanliness should be peremptorily insisted upon, nor should any impurities be thrown or otherwise allowed to collect near the lines: the best plan for compassing this end, is to place a Maistry, Duffadar or Cangany in charge, fining him when a breach of the rules is observed.

Coolies should sleep on *raised* beds or charpoys, they will gladly do so if they are supplied with a few planks. Each division of the lines should have a door on wooden pivots.

Lines should be repeatedly coated with mud to keep them in repair, and plastered with liquified cowdung, which latter destroys vermin, and is exceedingly clean when dry. No interstices or cracks in the mud should be left open, or these will become terribly infested with fleas, more especially if the lines be left untenanted for a short time. An occasional coat of chunam whitewash will also be of advantage in discouraging vermin, and rendering the atmosphere within wholesome.

The coolies should be encouraged to make little gardens, cultivating for their own use, brinjals, Indian corn, beans and other vegetables: to attain this without much loss to the proprietor, and for other reasons (such as the coolies keeping sheep, pigs, and other animals), the lines should be built on grass hills or waste open land, and not on the part of the estate planted with coffee.

With regard to the number of rooms or divisions in each set of lines, 20 is as many as is advisable, if so many they should be arranged in a double row, back to back. I am of opinion that small sets of 6 or 8 compartments are the best, as the different castes are not then so likely to come in collision, nor the people to annoy each other. Moreover, small sets of lines are better, as, should one catch fire and be destroyed, the loss and inconvenience would not be so considerable, as in the case of a large set; for the same reason there should not be a great number of sets of lines built in one locality, to prevent a conflagration spreading.

When we consider the number of fires which burn nightly in every set of well filled lines, without flue or chimney to conduct the smokes and sparks to the outer air, and also the combustible nature of the lines, it appears not a little surprising that so *few* accidents by fire do occur. If a thatched building does in these hot climates catch fire, particularly in the dry season, it is *almost impossible* to extinguish the flames; indeed, the only resource is to destroy a portion of the building to create a gap between the unburnt portion and the flames.

CHAPTER XV.

TOPPING—HANDLING—PRUNING.

"TOPPING" is the term applied to that operation of pruning which is the first that is performed on young trees, to check their upward growth : in England this work is named "heading down." Topping is undertaken with various objects, the chief one being to force the plant to throw out strong and vigorous, lateral fruit-bearing branches ; another object is to prevent the tree growing too high for the coolies, in all the operations they undergo.

The height at which trees have to be topped must be determined by the climate, soil, and aspect of the locality in which they are situated.

In *cold climates* or in *poor soils*, the trees will not naturally grow to any great size, and should be topped low, and planted at such distances apart, as will prevent any waste of ground.

In *exposed situations*, the soil being rich, the trees would perhaps grow sufficiently large, but if allowed to get high they would get much shaken by the wind, and the higher they are, the more, of course, they would be thus affected ; the trees should, therefore, under these circumstances, be topped low, in a greater or less degree, according to the strength and violence of the wind, to whose influence they are subjected; where this is great and prolonged throughout the monsoon months, 2¼ feet or 2 feet will not be excessive. I have had occasion to have fields of young coffee, which were much blown in the S. W. monsoon, topped at 2 feet and 1½ feet, and found the result beneficial. At 1½ feet, a coffee plant would generally still have from 5 to 7 pairs of primary branches.

On *rich soil, aspect sheltered,* and the temperature warm and humid, or, in other words, in situations the most favorable to the growth and luxuriance of the coffee tree, the *maximum* height of 5 feet may be permitted. It must be recollected, however, that under few circumstances will such a combination of advantages be met with, as to warrant the adoption of such a height.

The important object of having the ground well covered must not be overlooked, nor must it be overdone, and it must always be borne in mind that the lower a tree is topped, the longer comparatively will be its side branches, or primaries, and vice versâ.

I do not consider that the height of a tree is other than a question of time, as regards its capability of producing leaves and fruit: the roots will take up a certain amount of nourishment from the soil; and this will be displayed, if not permitted to come forth in increased height, the tree will be compelled to vent its vigour and vitality in lateral bulk.

But the more bulky a tree is, the more ground it will occupy, hence it is more economical of space to grow high trees, and plant close; this only in moderation, and the latter mode will require a rich soil, and can only be practised in sheltered spots.

The great disadvantage of high trees, besides that alluded to in the commencement of this chapter, is, that their lower branches being in a great measure excluded from the benefit of light and air, by the mass of foliage above them, have a tendency to die off; and even when living to be weak and stunted from the same cause; such trees, when old, will frequently be seen to have lost all the lower branches, assuming somewhat the form of an umbrella. This can only be guarded against by careful and regular "handling," or hand pruning, as I shall hereafter describe.

Having taken all points into consideration, I have arrived at the conclusion, that under ordinary circumstances, in topping, the average of 3 feet to $3\frac{1}{2}$ feet is the best height that can be adopted. Above $3\frac{1}{2}$ feet may be characterized as *high*, under 3 feet *low* topping.

Should trees have been allowed to grow too high, the defect can be easily remedied by a second amputation; should they have been topped too low, a sucker or young vertical shoot, being allowed to grow from beneath one of the top primaries will repair the error.

Topping should be performed as soon as the plant has attained the height desired, and can at this stage of the growth be best done by pinching off the green top with the finger and thumb. Should, however, the wood be matured at the height at which the trees are to be topped, a knife will be necessary.

For this work, each coolie should be provided with a measuring stick of the required length, and holding this against the stem of the plant from the ground upwards, he should take off the pair of primaries, next above the stick, close to the stem : the main stalk must then be cut through above the stumps of these. By this means the joint of the branches which have been cut off, will act as a band and prevent the stem subsequently splitting, by the strain caused by the weight of the next branches depending from either side.

I have heard it advanced, that coffee plants should not be topped too early, as it tends to force their growth ; but it must be remembered that the entire system of artificial cultivation, is a kind of forcing process, and it appears to me, that to permit a tree to grow a foot or so with leaves and branches, which are useless and subsequently to be cut off, is an absurd waste of sap, vitality, and *lime*.

In the commencement of this chapter, I stated that one of the objects aimed at in topping, was to compel the plants to throw out strong *primary* branches ; the next process to be described, "handling" or hand pruning, also greatly assists in producing this result.

After the primaries, the first branches which a tree produces are those which immediately come from the former, these are called "*secondaries*." These grow first, next to the stem, and it is apparent that if every primary were permitted to produce two or three pairs of secondaries within a few inches of the stem of the tree, the centre of the latter would become a mere disorderly mass, impervious to light and air ; and also that the sap being intercepted and divided into so many channels, would be insufficient to produce large, long, or healthy primaries. To obviate these results, all the young shoots, proceeding from the primaries within the space of

6 inches next the stem, must be cut off: the sap will thus proceed along the primary for a further distance, at which the secondaries must be permitted to grow, and an open space of one foot in diameter will be left down the centre of the plant, for the free circulation of air and the sun's rays, both of which are necessary in abundance to produce healthy vegetation.

Commenced at this early stage, "*handling*" is a very simple operation, and if steadily and regularly pursued, will always remain so, and the regularity with which the tree is handled will much facilitate the knife pruning, which will be undertaken after the tree has borne crop. In most cases, handling, however, will require the knife, and in *every* case, where a branch is taken off to make room for new wood.

In laying down fixed rules for "handling" and pruning, an exact description of the form and economy of the plant will be found most useful, to render those rules clear and intelligible; I cannot do better, therefore, than insert the following quotation*:— "The sapling rises, always bearing leaves, and afterwards boughs above them, by pairs or in axillary form, and opposite these boughs lengthen themselves in the same manner and proportion; and as they grow, they always end, as the trunk, in a sharp point, which divides itself into two leaves, which also spread out at a proper distance, and so on.

"In their turn, *secondary* branches shoot out, directly above every leaf of the primary ones. These make their

---
* An abridgement of the "Coffee Planter of St. Domingo, by Laborie."—Higginbotham: Madras.

growth as the former, and bear *tertiary* branches if the tree is luxuriant.

"Here a material observation is necessary, as it is in a measure the foundation of the whole system of lopping or pruning.

"The vertical sapling or trunk has been shewn, bearing its boughs or primary branches, in opposite pairs; so that the inferior (or lower) ones exhibit the figure of a cross with the superior (or upper), thus the four branches, spreading in four different directions; and this is necessary that the tree may be garnished all round, without being embarrassed. Exactly on the same principle of avoiding encumbrance, the arrangement of the secondary and tertiary branches is different. They are all placed by pairs, on both sides of the mother-branches, so that all spread out horizontally and with a direction in some measure towards the circumference. If any should grow upward or downwards, they would become intricate, and the tree embarrassed.

"Nature makes no such blunders; and if such happen to be the unintentional effects of art, art must redress them, as we shall see in its place. It must also be observed, that the tree being in its natural state, two branches seldom grow from the same leaf or bud.

"Now, I suppose the tree to be about four or five feet high.

"The boughs near the ground will extend wider, as they are nearer the source of vegetation, so that the shape of the tree is pyramidal. All those branches of three orders or more, garnish it richly, but as all are horizontal from below upwards, all diverging from the centre more or less, all placed either at the four faces of the trunk, (and these at distances at least eight or nine inches from each other at the same face) or both sides of the mother-branches, the profusion of Nature can neither be perplexed nor intricate."

All shoots produced by the main trunk, other than lateral branches, are known as suckers.

It must be always borne in mind that the main object of the pruner in all his operations, should be to preserve as much as possible the symmetrical arrangement of Nature above described; with the additional consideration, of endeavouring to obtain from the tree a richer and more vigorous yield of crop, than Nature, if left to herself, would cause it to produce. The objects of pruning are "the promotion of growth or bulk, lessening bulk, modifying form, promoting the formation of blossom buds, enlarging fruit, adjusting the stem and branches to the roots, removal of decayed plants or trees, and removal or cure of diseases."*

After having removed all the secondaries growing within 6 inches of the main trunk, on every primary, the next operation is to take off every alternate opposite secondary of those which remain on the main branch, leaving no pairs and *but one secondary only from each joint:* this greatly strengthens those which are left, as they naturally become more vigorous than if the sap which they thus receive were divided.† "As 'secondaries' left on too near the stem tend to weaken the 'primaries,' so do they, when left in pairs, cramp that expansion, which takes place under the treatment I advise."

---

* Rhind's History of the vegetable kingdom.
† W. on Pruning.

This done, nothing further is required on young trees, but to keep off the suckers, which will begin to appear shortly after topping, generally from beneath the junction of the top-most primaries and stem, though sometimes from many other parts of the trunk.

Suckers should always be pulled off by hand, and not cut off, in order that by the extraction of the root or germ, generally effected by the former method, future growth may be repressed.

Under the above treatment, the young tree will be in a condition for producing a maiden crop. This will probably come principally from the primaries, and from the oldest part of the first secondaries on the lower part of the trees. While crop is ripening, every assistance should be given the trees, by keeping off any useless or superfluous shoots. After the crop, commence pruning again : at this stage of the trees, growth, the rule to cut off all secondaries that have borne crop does not, in my opinion, apply, as in all probability they have produced fruit from a few joints only, near the main branch, in which case they should be left to bear another season.

If the distances between the joints be great, tertiary branches, under some circumstances, are permitted to grow in the same order as the secondaries, or alternately on opposite sides. But if the trees are close-jointed and the primaries and secondaries numerous, "tertiary" branches, as a rule, are better dispensed with altogether.

The criterion of good pruning, is the production of *annually equal* good crops, as well as the preservation of the trees in health, symmetry, and vigour.

To ensure average crops annually, the above system must

be carefully followed out, changing the sides on which the secondaries are taken off, one side producing crop on the secondary of the previous year's growth, while the opposite eye is producing a shoot for the production of the subsequent year's crop. This is a simple system, and one which, if accompanied by frequent and *careful* handling, will produce the most satisfactory results.

One old Ceylon Planter has, I believe, his estates handled once a month, but from what I have seen of the growth of wood in most districts, I should not suppose so often as this to be necessary. Once in every two or three months, done by careful hands, would be sufficient.

All shoots having an *inward, upward,* or *downward* tendency, in fact all those which are not proceeding in the order described before, should be early removed—especially those crossing others, or tending to fill up the open space in the centre of the bush. When more shoots than one proceed from a single eye, the strongest and most promising one should be selected, and the others removed.

As I have before observed, regular and systematic handling ensures easy pruning, and when the latter is undertaken after the crop, take off the secondary branches which have fully borne, taking care to leave enough wood for the next season's crop: to do so, you may sometimes be obliged to leave some that has already borne. The tendency of heavy pruning is to make a tree throw out quantities of new wood; this has a weakening effect, and must not be done unnecessarily; if, however, previous neglect renders recourse to this necessary, follow up the pruning with immediate handling to suppress excessive and superfluous growth.

The more weak and bare a tree is, the less its vital powers can bear a "cutting up," and the more healthy and well-trained, the less it will require such treatment.

Heavy pruning, moreover, should never be resorted to without the application of manure, to enable the tree to answer the calls made on its strength.

When estates have been neglected or badly pruned for a long period, the planter should not try and reform the trees all at once, but rather extend the period of discipline over two or three seasons; because cutting the trees into shape will not only cause the planter to lose one or two crops, but will be so exhausting to the trees, that they take a long time to recover, and many will die.

In commencing to prune a tree which has been allowed to become an almost impenetrable mass, the first thing to be done is to open out the centre, take off all the suckers, and then the branches can be examined and a liberal selection of wood made.

As a rule, primaries should never be cut at all, except in cases where they have become very long, whippy, and drooping; under these circumstances, the end may be docked or cut off below some good secondary, and the latter substituted as the leader. But primary branches should never be cut on the grounds of their having become leafless, or sickly, a secondary should rather be removed that its parent branch may have more sap. If the end of a primary has died, there is no harm in breaking off the part that is dry and rotten, but it is better to leave it than to allow coolies to get into the habit of cutting primaries at all : if left, it will only die back to the next healthy secondary, which having been previously left on the above-mentioned system of selection, will naturally supply its place.

Above all, be careful in pruning and do not hurry your pruners inordinately, it is better to get a little of this work done carefully and with deliberation, than to get the pruning finished, badly and slovenly, by the 15th of February, a date which is early for the completion of this work; indeed, it is seldom much before that the entire crop will have been gathered. In Ceylon, "handling and pruning" is generally estimated to cost about 18*s.* to £1 per acre per annum.

On old estates where the trees have become very "shuck" and scraggy, a new impetus may often be given to them by sawing off a foot or more of the stem, accompanied by a good manuring, and in this case, if desirable, a sucker may be permitted to rise to compensate for the decrease in height.

CHAPTER XVI.

MANURING.

The object of manuring is the improvement of soil rendered poor by excessive culture, and this is done by the introduction into it of substances or properties, in which it has become deficient.

Some soils are naturally poorer and less productive than others, but as manuring is generally an expensive job, and at all times a work of time and labor, it is obvious that a good rich soil which will yield a succession of crops, without assistance, is the most economical to purchase.

It is a mistake, however, to suppose that any soil, however rich, will yield a succession of the same crop, for any length of time, without assistance, in the form of manure; though good virgin forest soil should not require any manure until, at any rate, after the second crop. Poor land, such as " Chena," Raggee patches and grass hills, really require manure the very first season; hence they are seldom planted with coffee.

The subject of *manuring* has been considered so important from the earliest times, that many of the old writers have given much practical information respecting it. Theophrastus strongly recommends digging and stirring the ground. Xenophon recommends the ploughing in of green plants, " for such," he says, " enrich the ground as much as dung ;" he also recommends enriching land by introducing into it earth from the bottoms of rivers and canals. Cato also strongly indicates the necessity for digging up and manuring cultivated lands.

The point most to be considered with reference to this subject, is the manner in which the greatest amount of the constituent part of plants, which have been wasted by an excessive fruitfulness, produced by artificial cultivation, can be restored to them through the soil.

Of what then do plants consist ? We are informed, of hydrogen, oxygen and nitrogen, with carbon and some few earthy salts ; and, therefore, bodies containing the greatest amount of these constituents, arranged in such a manner as may be suitable for absorption by the roots and leaves of plants, are the best adapted to be used as manures.

Decaying animal and vegetable substances, and a few mineral productions, make up the various manures used in every cultivation, and the more fluid or gaseous the nutritious parts of these substances are, the most easily they will be absorbed by the plants. Mr. Rhind says,*—" The great object therefore in the application of manure should be to make it afford as much soluble matter as possible to the roots of the plants, and that in a slow and gradual manner, so that it may be entirely consumed in forming its soft and organized parts."

Substances which are composed, for the most part, of mucilage, gelatinous or fatty fluid, are those which contain

---

* History of the vegetable kingdom.

nearly all the elements of life in vegetation, in their normal state; as these are always combined with masses of woody fibre, a chemical change is necessary to render them food for plants.

Animal matters decompose more readily than vegetable, and glutinous, albuminous more quickly than woody fibre.

"Whenever manures consist principally of matter soluble in water, the too rapid putrefaction to which they are liable, must be prevented as much as possible: the only circumstances under which fermentation is required being, when the manure contains a great proportion of woody fibre."

To promote decomposition, moisture and the action of an atmosphere from 55 to 80 degrees are necessary, besides the existence of sugar, mucilage, starch, &c.

To prevent decomposition, manures should be kept dry and cold, and protected from the atmosphere.

Green vegetation being that manure which is generally the most ready to hand, and the most easily applied, deserves the first notice. The best method of applying it, is to dig it into the soil when in flower, or just before arriving at that stage: the more juicy and soft it is, the sooner green vegetation should be buried after its death, as the decomposition will go on *more gradually* under the ground, than when exposed to the air; it should not, however, be turned in too deep, as fermentation, to separate the woody fibre it contains, will then be entirely prevented by the exclusion of *air* and compression.

Woody fibres, such as bark, saw-dust, shavings, &c., are useless as food for plants, unless decomposition has been caused: this can be done, by their being brought into contact with some substances which will act the part of mucilage, saccharine matter, or starch, or with lime.

Wood-ashes when containing charcoal, and not too much burned, is useful as manure. *Charcoal* has the property of absorbing oxygen and becoming carbonic acid.

On Wood-ashes, Mr. Wall of Ceylon, states,—"I have used wood-ashes with marked advantage. This manure has the advantage of being both cheap and abundant. As *we* use the ashes, they contain much soluble alkaline matter, which, in England, is almost always previously abstracted for the manufacture of soap. For this reason, ours are particularly valuable, and cannot fail, when judiciously used, to give very beneficial results."

Dead bodies of animals, when buried under five or six times their bulk of earth, and one part of lime, impregnate the surrounding earth, so as to make it excellent manure, after the lapse of two or three months. This is worthy of remembrance, as cattle frequently die on estates, and each might thus be converted into a large quantity of manure of the richest and most nutritious kind.

Poonac, being a vegetable substance which contains much oily matter is a valuable manure; its effect is however to produce wood and leaves rather than crop. Before applying, it should be moistened and pulverized; it should then be put in small trenches close to the roots of the trees, and well mixed with the earth till the trench is filled. It is more adapted for hot than cool climates, as in the former its oily part is more soluble.

Ten cwts. an acre of Poonac applied in the proportion of

about one quart of the powder to each tree, will produce, in a few months, a fine shew of healthy green wood.

Bones, containing as they do, a large proportion of earthy salts, such as phosphate of lime, (one of the component principles of the coffee bean), magnesia, and carbonate of lime, as well as fat, gelatine, &c., are an excellent manure. They must be first ground up into powder and then applied in the same manner as *Poonac*, and in order that they may act with full effect, the soil should be dry.

As *bones* tend to produce crop rather than leaves and foliage, they are most advantageously applied, in combination with poonac.

Mr. Wall thinks, that the effect of one application of *bones* should be apparent for six years, and that one pint, per tree, or five cwts. per acre is sufficient.

Guano is the excrement of sea birds which live on animal food; and is brought from the Islands of China, Ilo, Iza, and Africa, in the South Sea.

When exhibited for manuring purposes it has the appearance of fine, brown powder. It contains ammonia, uric acid, potassa, phosphoric acid, a little fat and sand.

Guano is a most valuable manure, its effect is to produce both foliage and fruit, but it is best applied with some more bulky substance, such as *Poonac*.

Sal ammoniac and other mineral salts are all valuable manures entering as they do, largely into the constituent part of vegetables, but Mr. Wall observes, "that their solubility and affinity for water makes them liable to be carried down below the reach of the roots, or swept away by rain before they have been absorbed."

The best method of applying Sal Ammoniac is in combination with woody fibre or jungle, which it rapidly assists in decomposing.

Coffee Pulp. Of this I have not a very favorable opinion, as I have not observed much benefit derived from its application, except for a few months.

Possibly, were it applied *fresh*, it would gain a different character, and, indeed, it must contain sugar, mucilage and other properties which in themselves are useful as food for plants. Applied fresh, it would operate in much the same degree as green herbage, decomposing gradually if applied near the surface, and becoming matter easily absorbable by the roots.

Thatch Grass, when green, should be applied, but, consisting as it does, principally of fibrous matter, is of itself but little use as manure, but when put in with cowdung or other matter to dissolve the fibre, it will be beneficial. In any case, however, mana grass is useful to keep the soil loose and free when buried in it.

Mr. Wall considers it an excellent plan, to lay a stratum of grass on the surface of the ground, in situations which are cold, wet and bleak, as it causes the ground to retain heat, and prevents wash. He says,—" I have applied it to a cold, heavy, yellow soil, in which coffee bushes could scarcely exist, and where their scraggy branches had only a few small yellow leaves on them, and the effect was most surprising. Not only were the trees soon clothed with fine dark green foliage, but even the soil appeared to be changed, and to the depth of 3 or 4 inches, became friable and dry."

This ground thatching I have myself tried, and found it very beneficial in repressing the growth of weeds, besides the results above described by Mr. Wall ; but I must warn the planter against the danger of fire which it causes, as a spark falling on this thatch in the dry weather might set a field of coffee in a blaze, and cause immense damage.

Cattle dung is a manure universally known and used, it contains nearly the same ingredients as vegetable substances when in a state of fermentation, absorbing oxygen, and producing carbonic acid gas.

There appears to be some diversity of opinion as to the manner in which cattle dung should be treated previous to application.

Sir Humphrey Davy was of opinion that only slight fermentation was necessary to render the product of the dunghill suitable for the use of the farm or garden. He says, "it is better that there should be no fermentation at all, before the manure is used, than that it should be carried too far."* In violent fermentation of the dung much of the gaseous matter is lost, which, had it been retained in the soil, would have been useful food for plants, and it has appeared to me that the fresher the manure when applied to the soil, the more eminently successful have been the results.

I have occasionally been astonished at seeing the reckless manner in which valuable manure is sometimes wasted, simply by exposure in heaps to the sun ; and at other times to observe coolies carefully collecting old cattle droppings off the grass hills, in the vicinity of coffee estates, those droppings being in that condition called (in Tartary, I believe) " Argols"† when they are eminently useful as fuel, but by

---

* Loudon's Encyclopædia of Gardening.
† See M. M. Huc and Gabet's Travels in Tartary.

the evaporation and decomposition, rendered totally unfit for use as manure, unless decomposed by the aid of lime.

English farmers prefer using manure considerably fermented, until it gets into the state they call "short muck," or a "soft cohesive mass" in such a condition that it may be cut by a spade ; on the ground that in this state dung contains more *humic acid,* which, with carbonic acid gas, constitute the chief food of plants, according to Mr. Loudon, who says,—" It has been *proved* that rotted dung contains more *humic* acid and carbonic acid gas, weight for weight, than *fresh dung.*"

If we draw a line between the excessive decomposition required by Mr. Loudon and the theory of Sir Humphrey Davy, we shall probably arrive at the true point as to the degree of fermentation required.

Manure must never be exposed to the sun or wind, as most of its useful properties will then be lost, and by excessive evaporation and fermentation the fibres of the vegetation on which the living animal fed, only will remain.

Mr. Loudon describes a method of manufacturing and using liquid manure, practised by the farmers of German-Switzerland.

The animals are stalled on a boarded floor, having a downward inclination of four inches to the hinder part of the cattle, whose excrements fall into a gutter behind, which is fifteen inches deep and ten inches wide.

This gutter is so formed as to be capable of receiving, at pleasure, water supplied from a reservoir; the trench communicates with five pits or holes, which can be opened or shut at pleasure, and are covered over with a floor of boards to facilitate the fermentation. These pits should be water-tight to prevent infiltration, and there should be five of them, in order that the liquid may be left undisturbed to ferment for four weeks, and one pit must be closed up every week.

Every evening water is let into the gutter, and in the morning the cattle-keeper carefully mixes with the water the excrement which has fallen during the night, breaking up all lumps, and forming the whole into a liquid of uniform density : on the manner in which this part of the operation is performed, mainly depends the quality of the manure.

The best proportion of the mixture is three-fourths water and one-fourth excrement.

Dr. Shortt recommends the use of a pit communicating with the cattle shed, into which the dung and urine of the cattle should be emptied ; this pit must be thatched over, and all the rubbish of the house, lines, &c., such as dust, ashes, offal, &c., thrown in ; once a week a layer of lime should be sprinkled over these impurities, followed by an inch of earth.

An excellent coffee planter in Ceylon, adopts the following plan : the cattle shed, an oblong building, with a properly plastered floor sloping to one side, at about 6 inches in 10 feet, has along its entire length, a manure pit into which all the bedding and excrement is daily emptied, the pit is of course under roofing, and in it are kept a number of pigs, fed on green grass, chick weed, &c., and poonac ; their continual tramping on the entire mass of cattle bedding with their little sharp hoofs, shortly renders the whole into an extremely rich and compact mass, short and easily cut with the mammotie when it is desirable to empty the pit.

In order to keep the pigs in health, it will be necessary to throw in a considerable quantity of bedding daily, and if possible, have clean spaces round the pit for them to sleep in at night.

The plan I have always myself followed is simply as here described. The cattle shed, is a large oblong building, having the floor excavated to the depth of 3 or 4 feet below the surface of the ground; in and around this, bricks are laid down, pointed and tarred as well as the sides as high as the surface of the ground outside: clean bedding is laid down all over the floor, the cattle are turned in for the night (being allowed to graze out all day), and green grass laid all round the walls as night fodder. Every morning the cattle are turned out to graze, and before their return in the evening, a fresh layer of green bedding, of sufficient thickness to keep the cattle dry and clean when lying down, and night fodder, is laid down over that of the previous day, leaving the former deposits undisturbed.

This system may go on for any length of time, until the manure has risen 2 or 3 feet above the level of the outside ground, when it will be 6 or 7 feet in depth, and the cattle may then be turned into another shed, and the former one emptied.

By the above course, a rapid decomposition is prevented, by the exclusion of air, and yet sufficient fermentation to render the manure easy of application, is promoted, carbonic acid gas is formed, and at the end of six or nine months when the shed is emptied, the manure will be found fragrant, fresh, and moist.

The only objection I have heard advanced against my

plan is, that this mode of keeping the cattle would be apt to render them unhealthy; but this is not the case, always provided that a sufficiency of clean bedding is supplied to them every day. After three years' experience of this treatment of over one hundred head of cattle, I am inclined to think, that the deep warm bed under them, rather tends to promote their healthfulness than otherwise.

On Estates in the vicinity of a public road, manure should be collected as fresh as possible, and preserved in a cool dry shed until required.

In applying manures to the soil, there are one or two points to be considered: first, the position in which they will be most easily reached by the roots of the plants; and second, the way in which they may be best retained in that position; and third, the manner in which they may be the most economically distributed.

Cattle-shed manure, or, in fact, manure of any kind, when intended for the benefit of the coffee plants, should not be put more than one foot beneath the surface of the ground, as it is within a stratum of little over that depth that the principal feeding fibres of the plants roam in search of nourishment.

On flat land, *where there is no danger of wash,* undoubtedly the best manner of applying manure is to spread it, well broken up, generously and of uniform quantity over the ground, and then dig it well in with a pick, delving to the depth of a foot. Flat land, however, is not often met with on coffee estates, and, therefore, on the slopes, continuous horizontal trenches between each horizontal line of trees answer the best. These trenches should be one foot deep on the lower side, the bottom level, and fifteen inches wide.

A man may be set to each line of trees, commencing at the foot of the hill, thus the length of the trenches he makes will be the same as the space between each row of trees, say five or six feet; of these, he will probably make from 20 to 30 a day in old land, void of roots, &c. When the first trench has been opened, place along the bottom of its entire length six inches deep of marna grass or jungle, or ferns, &c.; on this sprinkle the manure, at the rate of one basketful for each tree, breaking up all the lumps, and spreading it nicely over the grass, in the bottom of the trench: then the trench next above may be commenced, and the newly excavated earth rolling down will cover the manure.

Manuring in this manner is very costly, and I have found it amount to between £7 and £8 per acre, if applied at any distance from the cattle-shed; the results, however, will be remarkable, giving a probable increase of 5 to 6 cwts. per acre of crop for four years.

The usual method of applying manure is simply to dig a small hole above each tree near the roots, and to empty therein a basketful of dung, the hole being then covered over.

This, though a cheap way, is not advisable, as the ground is not sufficiently disturbed, nor the manure properly distributed, *whereby it is in a great measure wasted.* Manure should never be put in in great lumps or clods, as it breeds great quantities of worms, grubs, &c., many of which make fatal attacks on the trees.

For applying *pulverized manures* such as poonac, bone-dust, guano, ashes, &c., it will be evident that if they were spread over so much ground, at the rate of one pint or one quart per tree, their properties would become too much dispersed: the manner, therefore, of application, should be as follows: dig a small hole about one foot wide, ten inches deep on the lower side, and a foot and a half long—if on a slope, *above* the tree—about one foot from the stem: into this hole sprinkle first with the hand a little of the powdered manure, then a little earth, again some manure, then some more earth, and so on, until the allowance for that tree is completed; by this means, the manure is preserved and immediately brought into use.

If Poonac is not carefully pounded and used as above, the jungle pigs root it out as food.

A simple method of manuring, consists of digging a good sized hole or trench between every four trees, and leaving it open to receive any leaves, weeds, sticks, &c., that may fall into, or be scraped into it, "the soil taken out should be spread over the roots of the trees, to cover any denuded roots there may be. * * * * They form reservoirs for much valuable matter, which would otherwise be dispersed and lost." *

---

* Mr. Wall's Essay.

CHAPTER XVII.

DISEASES.

LIKE the members of the animal kingdom, all classes of plants are liable to suffer from diseases, and subsequently to succumb to the great destroyer—Death. They have likewise numerous enemies, which prey upon them in various ways, more or less deleterious and subversive of the objects with which they are cultivated. They, therefore, require that assistance and protection to obviate these evils, which the advance in a knowledge of the physiology of vegetation, has placed within the reach of the cultivator.

Some diseases arise from a derangement of the circulation of the fluids; brought about from different causes. Others from an undue absorption of water; others, doubtless, are produced by the influences of climate; and some from injuries by various kinds of insects. The diseases of plants are divided by Tournefort into the following classes; first, those which arise from too great an abundance of sap; second, from having too little; third, from its bad qualities; fourth, from its unequal distribution; and fifth, from external accidents.

Too much sap is produced in situations where the climate is too moist, and where is too great a quantity of rain. But cattle dung is supposed to be a preventive of those diseases which are caused by a superabundance of moisture.

The best remedy where plants suffer from want of moisture or nourishment, is to keep the ground free of weeds, pulverize the soil, and protect them by shade.

The principal diseases resulting from external causes, to which the coffee plant is subject, are caused by BUG, WORM, STUMPS, ROT or BLIGHT, and GRUBS.

The Bug, *Coccus* coffeæ or *Lecanium* coffeæ, has been fully described by Mr. Nietner of Ceylon, in his valuable work entitled* " Enemies of the coffee tree." The pest may be divided into two classes, the *Black* and *White* Bug, being apparently two distinct species of insects, though both bearing the same name.

The *Black Bug* is a minute insect which fixes itself in myriads over the tenderest shoots of the plants, at first depositing countless eggs in small scaly formations, resembling scollop-shells on a rock ; each of these structures is a female bug, containing many hundreds of eggs, in a state of incubation.

After a time, a coffee tree will become entirely covered with these ; and a sootty, black powder, which is an excretion of the insect, makes a tree thus afflicted, easily discernable from some distance.

From one tree the bug will spread over whole fields, or whole estates ; the growth of the trees is much affected by it, the fresh shoots being always the first attacked, and such wood as there is, produces but little crop.

The crop on " Buggy" trees, is generally, all nipped off at

---

* This work is now out of print.

the stems of the berries in their early and tender stage, so that the damage which this blight effects, is most serious.

Dr. Shortt gives in his work, the following description of the coffee bug, taken from Sir J. Emerson Tennent's most valuable and useful work on Ceylon :—

"A number of small wart-like bodies may be seen studding the young shoots and buds, and, occasionally, the margins on the undersides of the leaves. Each of these warts is a transformed female containing a large number (700) of eggs, which are hatched within it.

"When the young ones come out of their nest they may be observed running about, and looking like woodlice ; shortly after being hatched the males seek the under-sides of the leaves, while the females prefer the young shoots as their place of abode. The larvæ of the males undergoes transformation in pupa beneath their own skins, their wings are horizontal, and the possessing wings may probably explain the comparatively rare presence of the male on the bushes.

"The female retains her power of locomotion till nearly her full size, and it is about this time, that her impregnation takes place.

"The coffee bug first appeared on the Luhallagalla Estate in 1843."

This scourge cannot be overcome and destroyed unless taken in a very early stage, and when it is found on a few isolated trees.

Each tree on which it makes its appearance being at once detected, it may be killed, by sprinkling over the parts affected, a mixture of pounded saltpetre and quicklime, in equal proportions.

A planter in Mercara informed me, that he and some other planters in Coorg, had tried with much success bathing the diseased parts with a mixture of :—Soft soap, tar, tobacco, and Spirits of turpentine in equal parts.

To keep the "bug" in check, each tree visited by the insect should be at once singled out, and treated with one or other of the above receipts. A cooly with a bucket and a piece of rag can perform the service effectually, and if one application is insufficient, a second or third will succeed.

In order to keep a constant look out, one or two persons might be profitably employed, for the above sole employment, once a single instance has been discovered.

From my own observations, I should say the black Bug prefers to frequent cold and wet situations. It generally first appears under shelter of a large boulder of rock, a belt of trees, or in some moist nullah.

A hot dry season appears occasionally to cause it to disappear, until the rainy season returns.

The black Bug will sometimes hang about an estate for one season only, sometimes for years, and then disappear as mysteriously as it came; though on some high, cold, and wet situations it appears to delight to form its depôt and stronghold, and reside in perpetuam.

The *white Bug*, I imagine to be a distinct species of insect from the black Bug : it is a small insect about 1-16th part of an inch in size, of an oval, flat form, with parallel ridges running across its back from side to side. It is quite white, and forms a flowery deposit at the roots of the leaves and round the stems of the blossom groups, which it cuts off either in that stage or later, when the young berries are formed as the case may be ; and its presence may easily be known by the large quantities of small green fruit, which, in the proper season, may always be seen under every tree attacked by it.

The second prescription recommended for use, in the destruction of black Bug will also be found useful for destroying this, if applied in the same manner, though a simple solution of tobacco will be more easy of application.

Differing in its tastes from the black Bug, this blight is more injurious in hot, dry situations, generally disappearing entirely towards the end of the wet season, only, however, to appear again, after blossom, at which time it does the most damage.

The Worm is a disease but too well known in Wynaad, and it is more or less prevalent throughout all the coffee districts of Southern India, though, as far as I have seen, but little met with in Ceylon.

It is also called the *coffee fly*, as this is one of its forms of existence, when it appears as a long, shining, hard black and yellow fly, supposed, I believe, to be sometimes also red-and-black.

These insects bore a hole in the stem of the coffee tree, forming a passage by which they proceed right through into the centre of the stem ; and they therein deposit the larvæ.

Their presence is only to be discovered when the tree begins to droop, and subsequently dies down to the part of the trunk where the insect has effected its entrance, at which the trunk can be easily broken off by a slight pull to one side ; and the best course is destroying, if possible, the upper portion which contains the worm, as the insect always works *upwards.*

Below the fracture, new shoots will probably make their appearance, which can be trained if desired.

Notwithstanding the severity of this scourge, I have not been able to gather any scientific information relating to it, though it much resembles some beetles, described as attacking fir plantations in Europe, in the same manner. I am unfortunately, quite unable to say, where, in what form, or in what season the insect is most assailable, and thus I can advise no remedy for its destruction, except this, that as experience shews that it is most prevalent on weedy and neglected estates, the best way to keep it out, will doubtless be to keep the estate free from weeds.

When on a short visit to Coorg, a gentleman residing on the Mangalore ghaut shewed me quite a new form of blight, which I had never before heard of, which he assured me caused much mischief in that district.

This disease may be termed *stump,* and operates as follows :—The stump of a certain class of tree causes, *when beginning to decay,* the death of all the coffee trees in its immediate vicinity. The remedy for this only lies in the removal of the stump in question. ROT or *Blight* is known to exist when the young leaves and shoots turn black and wither. This is usually caused by too much wet, cold, or dampness of soil. Drain well, and thatch the ground two or three inches deep with grass—if possible.

Grubs.—Coffee trees, previously the finest in a field, often die off suddenly in localities where the soil is rich and full of organic matter, or has been heavily manured.

A gentleman, many years ago in Ceylon, determining to have an extra fine field of coffee, after pitting, half filled each of the holes with manure. To his surprise, in the second year, some 25 per cent. of his trees died; determined to ascertain the cause, he dug out all the dead trees, and found that they were all eaten at the roots by large yellowish grubs. These insects always congregate in decaying matter. The best remedy for destroying them is to dig deeply, and kill all that appear. This is also one of the reasons why manure should not be put in in large clods, but should be broken up and *distributed* through the soil.

Rats, especially that called the Golonda Rat, are very mischievous, biting off young branches and the stems of young plants, in some parts doing incalculable damage. They—as well as squirrels, monkeys, wild cats, &c., eat a great deal of the ripest coffee in crop time, and should, therefore, if possible be destroyed.

Large Grasshoppers, also as well as numerous other insects, do grievous damage in severing young plants near the roots, as well as biting off the twigs and branches of old trees; these insects cannot well be guarded against, but should be destroyed whenever found on the estate or in its vicinity. But for a further account of all enemies of the coffee tree, I cannot do better than recommend all persons interested in the subject to peruse the work, I before mentioned, of Mr. Nietner, a gentleman who has given the fullest consideration to the subject.

CHAPTER XVIII.

CROP.

THE grand result and end of all cultivations is consummated and attained when the crop is gathered off the trees.

The reader of the foregoing pages will perceive the number of works that have to be entered upon, the precautions to be taken, and the dangers which must be guarded against to gain this object with reference to the coffee tree. This being the case, I purpose now making a few remarks on the securing of the crop which every coffee planter hopes yearly to gather. In the end of December, numerous buds will begin to appear at every eye, on all the bearing wood, or the secondaries or tertiaries which have been purposely left for the coming crop in handling.

These having previously been properly selected, none of them will have to come off in the *pruning* which follows the *previous crop*. These buds will increase in size, having a greenish white and glossy appearance till March when the showers come down, they will then come whiter and fuller until about the 15th of March, when the whole estate will come out in full bloom. To describe the beautiful appearance of a fine heavy-bearing estate at this period is almost beyond my powers; ridge upon ridge, and wave upon wave of snowy fragrance, on a background of glossy green, present a most charming effect. There are generally two, sometimes three, blossoms in the season, but the principal one should come out early in March. After a day or two the flowers fade—the more *gradually* they do so, the better. A good shower of rain is then beneficial to wash off the faded flowers, and a sight still more refreshing to the eye of the practical planter will be presented in the numerous little fruit germs left behind.

These should have whitish fresh tips, and the spot from which the stamen grew, a healthy appearance—as should the tips of the young berries be black, they will not come to maturity.

Crop will generally be full sized in September, and will gradually, in October, turn yellow and begin to ripen.

"Picking" will now commence—first, perhaps, only with a few hands; but gradually, as the fruit begins to assume a reddish tinge, all hands will be set on to gather in as fast as possible, and this will probably continue till the end of January, in some districts, while in others the *full* of the crop is over in about a month.

The berries should only be gathered as they become fully ripe, the object being that the coffee shall command a high price in the market, as that which is most ripe will have the greatest amount of aroma when roasted.

It is said to be attributable to the peculiar manner in which the Arabs gather their crops, namely, allowing them to ripen and dry on the trees, which they then shake receiving the produce on outspread cloths and mats, that the price of Mocha, exceeds that of the coffee produced in any other part of the world. To gather the berries *as they ripen*, it will be necessary to go over the estate two or three times, as the crop seldom ripens all at once, except on very young trees.

Should the planter, however, be short handed, it is generally best to get in at once all berries sufficiently matured to permit of an easy separation, by the pulper, of the beans and pulp; time is thus gained, although the quality may be slightly deteriorated.

For picking, each person is furnished with two bags, called in cooly parlance a "sack" and a "cooty sack." The former should be sufficiently large to tie up at the mouth, when it contains $1\frac{1}{4}$ Imperial bushel; the latter should be not larger than to contain one-eighth of this quantity, as it is intended to be worn round the waist of the picker, as he proceeds with his work, and each handful of berries dropped into it: when the small bag is filled, it is emptied into the large sack, which is left on the nearest road.

Thus the picker knows when he has gathered the required quantity of fruit, by the number of " cootty saques" which he has emptied into the big bag.

In full crop, each picker is, in Ceylon, tasked to fill a box measuring $1\frac{1}{2}$ Imperial bushel once in the evening, and once at noon, or twice a day.

Men, women, and children are all paid alike at this work, at the rate of so much per bushel, (usually 4*d*. per box) the amount each person brings in being entered against his or her name in the pay book. In this way it frequently happens that while a strong powerful man can barely gather his 2 boxes, a sharp little boy or clever-fingered woman will easily do so.

Strong, willing men, good at most hard field work, often make bad " pickers;" these should be, therefore, selected for store work, such as curing, as grass cutters for the cattle, &c., so as not to discourage or make them dissatisfied.

In picking, care should be taken, if possible, not to pull out the stalks of the clusters from the parent branch, as, in doing this, a rent is made and the eye of later sprouts destroyed ; to prevent this, coolies should not be permitted to gather a group of berries together, even though all perfectly ripe.

Green berries, in passing through the pulper, not only lose their outer covering but the inner coat or " parchment" also comes off, as also the " *silver skin ;*" they are also usually broken, consequently they ferment and rot when wet, and are entirely wasted. Moreover, they spoil the appearance of the sample, however fine the parchment coffee may be, and shew careless work.

In a large crop where hands are few, and the weather wet, the berries are apt, when slightly over-ripe, to burst and drop off the trees ; should the ground be free of weeds, nearly all this fallen fruit may be gathered up ; but should it be covered with weeds, much loss will accrue.

On the other hand, in dry weather the berries will dry up, and remain on the trees for a long time ; these, when gathered, should be soaked and slightly fermented before passing through the pulper, or they will be cut and broken. On large estates where the cherry has to be carried a long way from the field where it is gathered, to the store, iron piping may be laid to shoot it down the hill, saving much time and labour in carriage. These pipes are usually made of galvanized iron, in 8 feet lengths, and are used in the following manner. The store works being at the foot of the hill, perhaps a mile from the end of the estate above, a receiving-cistern and shed are erected at the top of the hill, in a convenient situation; into the receiving-cistern, water is conveyed, and the cherry coffee is measured into it, as gathered from the adjacent fields. At the bottom of the cistern the spout enters, and is conveyed at an equable gradient down to the works. A man is placed in the cistern to regulate the quantity of coffee that is to go down, so that the spouting may not get filled up, or clogged. With an ordinary supply of water, 60 to 80 boxes an hour may, in this way, be transmitted.

In laying spouting, some care is necessary, so as to have the gradient as even as possible; as, if one portion be very steep, and the next but gradual, the coffee will jam up the spout; the same danger must also be avoided, by making all the curves as gradual as possible. It will also often be necessary, to raise the spouting on posts, to cross nullahs and hollows to the next rising ground. Where the spouting lies on the ground, it should be pegged down, to prevent its rolling, or becoming displaced; two stout stakes driven firmly into the ground, one on each side, crossing at the top, and tied together, will effectually answer this purpose.

That part of the cherry loft of the pulping house, into which the coffee is spouted, should have a grating, so that the water may pass through. Should water be scarce, that which is brought by the spouting may be rendered available either to assist the water wheel, or feed the pulpers.

As soon as ripe coffee arrives in the store, it should be pulped. If left in the cherry loft too long before being pulped, it will ferment, and the parchment become discoloured.

After pulping, it must be left in the vat or cistern for 36 or 48 hours, to allow sufficient time for the saccharine matter adhering to the beans to be dissolved.

The next operation to this, is washing. The coffee in the cisterns should now be well trampled out by the coolies, to separate from the beans any pulp which may still adhere to them; then the water may be turned in, and the whole contents of the cistern violently raked and turned about, until the latter is nearly full. By this process, all the light worthless beans and berries will float to the surface, whence they may be skimmed off in a basket or sieve, and thrown in a heap by themselves. Now all the dirty water must be let off, together with all the skins which will have drifted to the lower end of the cisterm. This water must run into a lower *grated* vat, where the skins and any stray coffee will be retained. The cistern must now be allowed partially to re-fill with pure water, and the same operation be repeated, gradually raking down with the escaping water the remaining skins. When the parchment is perfectly clean and white, and free from skins, the washing operation may be considered complete.

As soon as coffee is washed, it should be carried up and spread out on mats, or on a clean barbecue to dry in the sun, being frequently turned about to get dry as soon as possible.

Before being despatched in bags, the parchment should be dried for three full days, as otherwise it will be apt to heat on the journey to the coast; but probably before carts or bullocks can be procured to convey it away it will have to be kept for some time in store; under such circumstances, it must be attended to with some care. It should be studiously preserved from damp, and frequently turned, so that it may all be exposed to the air.

In Ceylon, where the weather is always more or less uncertain, especially in crop time, it is necessary to keep a sharp look-out on the clouds, so as to get the coffee under cover, before a shower of rain comes down; as, once the parchment has dried, any subsequent wetting, seriously injures the quality.

But in Wynaad, so dry is the weather at this season, that many planters build no store at all, merely piling up the coffee in heaps on the barbecues after being perfectly dried. This is very different from Ceylon, where I can recollect six weeks of ceaseless rain in the midst of crop. The anxieties and worry of that period I shall never forget; I had myself 3 or 4,000 bushels of wet coffee piled up all over the drying ground; some of my neighbours had *more*. The only resource was constantly turning it over, night and day, to prevent its fermenting; but, in spite of all our endeavours, I recollect much of the coffee had sprouted at the tops, like potatoes. We were surprised and gratified subsequently, by finding in the price list, that the quality of the coffee had not suffered.

Mr. Clerihew's invention is adapted to be of immense benefit in a case like this, and it is now brought into use on most of the old estates in Ceylon. This is a system which dries coffee, by heat, under cover, and also draws a current of fresh air, either hot or cold, through the entire heap of coffee in the store, whereby the necessity for shovel or hand turning is obviated, and the coffee kept perfectly fresh and sweet.

CHAPTER XIX.

STORES, PULPING HOUSES, AND MACHINERY.

On all Estates, for the proper curing, and preparing for despatch of the crop, as also for its safe-keeping while still on the estate, certain buildings are required, such as stores and pulping-houses. As the first that comes into requisition is the Pulping House, it merits the first description.

This building must comprise three distinct compartments—namely, the *Cherry Loft*, the *Pulping Platform*, and the *Cisterns*.

The *cherry loft* is the receptacle or chamber into which the ripe coffee is emptied when brought in from the field, and must be *above* the pulpers, so that the coffee will fall, or can be conveyed by water into them. The *Platform* on which the machinery stands must be *above* the *cisterns*, into which the coffee is to run, after undergoing the operation of pulping.

The *cisterns* should be three in number—that is, two receiving-cisterns, each of such a size as to be capable of containing the largest amount of coffee that can be brought in, in any one day; and one washing cistern, into which the pulped coffee may be removed from the receiving cisterns, to be washed. All the cisterns should be so placed that the water they contain may be easily drained off, when desirable.

The most important consideration in the selection of a site for a pulping-house, is an ample supply of water, as this element is necessary for both the operations of pulping and washing, and should, if possible, be available also for turning the machinery.

The pulping-house should be erected in the vicinity of the main stream, so that water may be conveyed, at least 10 feet, above the level of the pulping platform; in this manner a 20-feet water wheel may stand on its axle at that level; should there be no large stream, however, its absence may, in most cases, be supplied by a dam of adequate dimensions.

The operation called "pulping," consists in separating the skin or pulp from the beans. This is done by the common pulper, and divers new inventions on the same principle.

The pulper consists of a framework of iron or wood, in which is fixed a revolving cylinder, covered with a sheathing of punched copper, like an enormous nutmeg grater. This cylinder, about 1 foot in diameter, and 2 feet in length, revolves inwardly towards two bars, called chops, iron-coated, one placed above the other, leaving a space of about $\frac{5}{16}$th of an inch between them. The upper chop is shaped in such a manner, that its upper edge is much further from the cylinder than the lower one, in order that the fruit may readily enter between it and the cylinder; which, in revolving, compresses the berries, forcing the beans out of them, which then pass out in front over the upper surface of the next chop. The pulp, on the contrary, being pierced by the rough points of the copper, adheres to the cylinder, and is carried in its revolution past the lower chop, the space between which and the cylinder, being too narrow to allow the beans to pass. The lower chop, it is needless to say, must be just so near the cylinder as to forbid the entrance of the coffee beans, while it admits all the pulp.

From the pulper, the coffee runs into the sieve, whence such berries as have not been properly acted upon in the first operation, are returned to it a second time. The pulp runs off at the back to a pit, where it is preserved for manure.

Another machine very much employed on large estates, in conjunction with the pulper, is the crusher. As its name designates, its operations consist simply in crushing the berry with such force as to cause a separation between the bean and pulp of the larger berries, while it softens the smaller ones, and makes them more easily acted upon by the pulper. It consists of a series of steel plates, overlying each other on a cylinder. Where it is used, the coffee passes into it first from the cherry loft, then into the sieve, whence such beans as have been pulped by it, pass through to the vats, and the remainder of the coffee is passed up into the pulper, either by hand, or by a most ingenious arrangement of buckets attached to revolving chains, which scoop up the coffee of the floor, and in revolving, carry it up and overturn it into the pulper. The crusher is, I believe, the invention of J. Brown, Esq., of Ceylon.

Butler's pulper is a very complete instrument, dispensing, as it does, with both chops and sieve. It consists of two cylinders covered with grooved metal, which revolve inwardly. When all the coffee is perfectly *fresh* and *ripe*, it answers very well, but where there are green or black berries, it crushes and injures them. It also requires great power in working, is rather difficult to set and keep in order, and is more expensive than the ordinary machine.

The following is by a Ceylon Planter on the subject of Pulpers generally, written about 1860 :—

"Pulpers—until within the last few years, had undergone less change, and shewn perhaps less improvement, than any other branch of the Coffee Planters' business. We had the same old rattle trap machine, (a cylinder of about 1 foot in diameter, covered with punched copper, like a huge nutmeg grater, revolving against 2 bars of wood, faced with iron, called chops, which separated the pulp or skin from the parchment covered bean) from the earliest introduction of coffee cultivation into Ceylon with the modification of cast iron spur and fly wheel, for the wooden ones at just in use with belt and drum. Then came, about ten years ago, and almost simultaneously, the crusher of Mr. Brown, and the pulper of Mr. Wall. The former has generally worked well, where there is plenty of water, but without that it is found heavy, and, therefore, not much used. The latter, as an article of merchandize, we hear little of now ; and must therefore conclude that either it has not answered the expectation of its originator, (who, by the way, took out a patent for it), or that it is too dear to get into general use, or is eclipsed by the more recent inventions. After it, the late Mr. Thomas Affleck was engaged on a new pulper, which was by his friends expected to supersede all that had gone before it. Mr. Affleck's death stopped midway this invention. Thereafter, almost simultaneously, appeared in the field Mr. Butler, an old

West Indian Planter, who had been a few years on a coffee estate in this country, and Mr. John Gordon, of 3, Railway Place, Fenchurch Street, London, formerly Affleck and Gordon, Engineers, Kandy; and these are at present the chief rival competitors for fame and fortune. Mr. Butler's is a double cylinder covered with grooved brass of apparently a very simple construction, and which with coffee of a uniform size, is said to work well, and do its work with little damage. But where the coffee is green, or black, or unequal, it crushes or peels. These are the objections we heard urged against it last year in many quarters; and we found that several of our friends, ere their crop was half through, had discarded this machine and resumed the old common pulper. This year we have heard it is working better, and that all those set up by Mr. Butler in person did well. Doubtless, like every other new invention, experience has enabled its patentee to remedy defects and improve on the primitive model. It is to be regetted that poor Mr. Butler died, just at the time that prospects for a career of usefulness and profit were open before him. His former supporters, we understand, are to carry on the business: but they will have considerably to reduce the charge for one of those machines before they will ever come into common use. £50 is a large sum to pay for a single pulper. Gordon's, on the other hand, excepting the barrel and the breast, is slightly different from the old machine. At least, it approximates it near enough to admit of the breast (which is the great merit of this invention) being applied to any ordinary pulper at a trifling cost. In fact, for £8 we believe any pulper can be fitted with one of Gordon's breasts, which those who tried last year have pronounced to work well. One gentleman, of great experience and intelligence, informed us that to an old pulper which would scarcely work through 30 bushels an hour last year, he had applied Gordon's breast, and now easily gets 60 bushels an hour out of it, without cutting any thing perceptible, and without requiring a sieve. This adaptability of the breast, as well as the price of the whole machine only £32, will always give Gordon the advantage in the market—supposing the other merits of the two machines to be equal, and it is not for us to say whether they are or not; each has its own admirers, and a little more experience will doubtless convince the planting community which is the preferable implement. For our own part, we prefer Gordon's as simple in construction, easy of application, cheap in price, and, as far as we have yet seen, sufficient for every purpose by land or water.

There are one or two others yet on the tapis, the invention of private planters; but, as neither has yet come before the public, it would be premature to notice them as inventions."

Since the above was written, Mr. Walker, of Walker and Co., Bogambra Mills, has brought out his little machine, which has met with much favor and success; it is called the "Disc-Pulper" and is exceedingly light, portable, and easily worked. I have been given to understand that the work of this pulper is very satisfactory and good.

For my own part, however, I should always prefer the old pulper, with crusher, circular sieve, and buckets, to any other arrangement of machinery I have yet seen or heard of for the performance of pulping; these, worked by a 20-feet over-shot wheel, will work off 180 *bushels* of fruit, per hour, (double pulpers of course), not cutting or pricking more than 3 or 4 per cent. if well set; a man and boy are sufficient to attend it in full operation : what more can be desired ?

In erecting *stores*, any material may be used which is of sufficient strength and indestructibility. I should say brick would be as good as any, excepting iron, of which, in galvanized, corrugated sheets, the best stores are made.

Iron stores are usually made 30 feet wide, and 100 or 120 feet long; they are laid down on a masonry foundation and frame-work, the floor being of iron gauze or coir matting stretched on reepers and joists. The great heat generated by the iron is very conducive to the preservation of the coffee.

Stores are usually made in two stories, the upper floor of joists, reepers and matting, thus a current of air may be made to pass through the coffee which is placed on it. The lower floor should be made of asphalte, as being strong, hard, smooth, and clean.

A clever invention for drawing a current of air through coffee placed on a mated floor was brought out by a Mr. Clerihew, and the apparatus now bears his name : I shall endeavour to describe intelligibly the manner in which this method is brought into action.

The *upper story* must have air-tight walls and roof, which must be closely joined together—the doors and windows should be of glass. The floor, on the contrary, is open, *i.e.* is made of coir matting, laid on one inch square reepers, laid one inch apart; these reepers, in their turn, are supported by joists.

It will be necessary that these joists lie lengthwise with the building, and on them, on the lower side, must be nailed ceiling cloth, well plastered with congee, and then whitewashed, to render it air-tight. This cloth will form the ceiling of the lower story, and above it, between it and the matting on which the coffee in the upper story is lying, will be a space of 6 or 9 inches, or the depth of the joists on which it is tacked. As the joists run lengthwise with the store, it will now be evident that there will be a clear passage between every two joists, (for the whole length of the store) and the ceiling cloth and the matting, of the whole length of the building.

At one end, partition off a portion of the lower apartment of the store, say 10 feet, by the entire width of the store, the sides of this chamber must be perfectly air-tight, only it must have *no ceiling*, for, the spaces before described between the coir matting of the upper story, and the ceiling of the lower must all open into it. In the end wall of this air chamber, leave an opening in which will be placed a pair of large fans, exactly like those of a winnowing machine. These fans are connected by a belt with the water-wheel and made to revolve rapidly, and in doing so they suck out a strong current of air from the inside, and as there is only one quarter from which the supply of air can be kept up, it is drawn through the coffee spread over the floor of the upper story.

This operation freely ventilates, and keeps fresh the coffee which has been dried. But for coffee which is still wet, hot air is required, which is produced in the following manner: at the opposite end of the building from the air chamber, on the ground outside, a furnace is erected, in the masonry, over the fire-place of which are inserted a number of iron tubes, one end of which are open to the air and the other enter the flue which communicates with the upper compartment of the store.

These tubes become heated by the fire, and a current of air passing through them becomes also heated, and rushes up the flue into the coffee room. The action of the fans at the other end of the building, combined with the want of any other means of escape, cause this hot air to pass entirely through the coffee, and it is finally cast away by the fans after its purpose has been effected.

The *fans* are thin iron plates on spokes, which, in rapidly revolving inwards, draw out the air from this chamber, and consequently through the whole of the upper floor on which the coffee is placed.

Even without hot air, this system without furnace, flue or air-tight upper story, will answer every purpose for keeping the coffee fresh, and will obviate any necessity for turning it over, which must otherwise be done once every day; for it will otherwise, without turning, unless perfectly dried, get musty, and ferment before it can be despatched.

Such expensive inventions as Clerihew's are hardly necessary in perfectly dry climates such as Wynaad, where the entire crop may, with perfect impunity, as regards preservation, be left heaped on the barbecue during the entire season, until despatched to the coast.

It is a great point for the rapid drying of coffee, to have ample barbecue room, or drying ground.

To facilitate the storage of the coffee on the approach of a shower, some planters use trays for drying the coffee in. These are usually light wooden frames 6 feet long by 2 feet broad, over the bottom of which is stretched coir matting or wire gauze. There should be a large shed adjacent to the drying ground for keeping these trays in, and when a shower of rain approaches, they can easily be piled one above the other, and be placed under cover in a very short time.

Good curing consists chiefly in having as few beans as possible, crushed, pricked, or injured by the pulper ; and in sending the coffee white, sweet, and clean to the coast.

To insure the former result, much attention and care must be paid to the " setting" of the pulper, that is to say, to the arrangement of the *chops* with reference to the cylinder, so that while they are placed sufficiently close to pulp expeditiously, they may not be near enough to the cylinder, or to each other to injure the coffee. The proper adjustment of the pulper may be attained in the following manner. In the commencement of the season "set" the pulper as nearly right as possible, then put a little coffee in with the hand and make the cylinder revolve. If the large berries only are pulped, the upper chop must be put closer ; if small berries are cut, place further out. If the pulp does not pass freely out behind, put the upper chop lower, and possibly the lower chop a little further from the cylinder. Allow ample space for the pulp between the lower chop and cylinder, but be careful not to leave so much as to permit the ends of the beans to enter, or they will be "bitten." Examine the pulp behind carefully, and see that no chipped or broken coffee is amongst it, if such be the case, too much space must be left somewhere ; if not between the lower chop and cylinder, then at the ends next the frame of the pulper.

The greatest nicety is required in placing the cylinder level in the frame, also in seeing that it is exactly and cylindrically turned ; that it, and also the ends of the chops, where their slope commences fit, and are perfectly flush with the frame. There ought to be no more space between the end of the cylinder and the frame, than just enough to enable the former to revolve freely without chafing; but even should it be so close as to chafe a little at first, it does not much matter, as it will soon wear down.

CHAPTER XX.

ESTIMATES, &C.

To the capitalist desirous of entering on coffee cultivation, some idea must be given of the cost of such an undertaking, and the probable returns which may be expected from the outlay.

The first outlay in the purchase of land can only be determined with any exactitude, when the locality of the future estate is decided on. Thus, in Ceylon land may cost any sum between £1 and £8 an acre. In Wynaad, the primary upset price of land is only the cost of survey; but it is subject to an annual tax of 2 Rupees in perpetuam, which tax, however, can be avoided by the payment of 25 years' rent, or Rupees 50 per acre, in advance; while land in the same district purchased from natives holding a "pukka" title can be had sometimes for Rupees 8, Rupees 10, or Rupees 12 per acre; the tax is then levied of Rupees 2 per acre per annum on all land under coffee cultivation only.

In Coorg, the Government terms are Rupees 2 per acre, and no tax for 5 years, but it would appear that there is but little that is suitable for coffee cultivation left at this date, it having been mostly taken up by Europeans some years ago who are now selling Rs. 30 to Rs. 40 per acre both bamboo land and forest.

Dr. Shortt in his estimates put the land down at Rs. 5 only, but I am not aware exactly where the application of his figures would be found possible.

Applying, then, an average of all these rates, *i. e*, in Ceylon, £1 to £8; in Wynaad, Rs. 8 to Rs. 50; in Coorg, Rs. 2 to Rs. 40; *Dr. Shortt*, Rs. 5, we get a sum of about Rs. 23-11-0, or £2-7-4½ per acre. I think, therefore, it will not be unfair to calculate on getting the land at about Rs. 25.

ESTIMATE—

For cost of purchasing 200 acres land in Wynaad, and bringing it into full bearing of Coffee; calculated on the basis of laborers' pay being 4 Annas per diem, men, and 2 Annas 8 Pie women and boys.

FIRST YEAR, *October 1st to September 30th.*

		RS.	A.	P.	RS.	A.	P.
Purchase of 200 acres at Rs. 25					5,000	0	0
Felling and clearing 50 acres at Rs. 20	B	1,000	0	0			
Tools. *Bill-hooks* 50, *Axes* 50, *Grass-hooks* 12, *Mamooties* 50, *Crowbars* 25.	C	300	0	0			
Cooly Lines, and Writer's hut	D	300	0	0			
Nursery of young plants for 2nd year's planting	E	250	0	0			
Roads (4 feet in the solid), 1 mile	F	120	0	0			
Lining and pickets	G	150	0	0			

	RS.	A.	P.	RS.	A.	P.
Pitting 50 acres, at 1,452 pits per acre, or at 5 feet × 6 feet each pit, 1½ feet cube.....	907	8	0			
Filling up the pits, *at* 120 *pits,* 4 *Annas*......	151	4	0			
Purchase of 72,600 plants, at Rs. 6 per 1,000.........	436	0	0			
Planting, at 200 for 4 Annas	90	12	0			
Cleaning up and first weeding, Rs. 6 per acre......... H	300	0	0			
Maistries' pay, 10 per cent. on coolie labor.............	327	0	0			
Writer's pay, Rs. 25 per mensem.....................	300	0	0			
				4,632	8	0
Contingencies..				463	4	0
	Rupees			10,095	12	0

(*B.*) Felling and clearing usually costs from Rs. 16 to Rs. 22-8 per acre ; on Bamboo land where a good burn is seldom obtained, the cost of clearing will be excessive ; but on forest land, on the contrary, the piling and subsequent burning would probably cost very little. The contract rates for " felling, clearing," and burning, are 30*s.* for the former, 15*s.* for the latter, or £2-5 in all.

(*D.*) Lines for the coolies will at first be only of a temporary character, as in this stage of operations it will not usually be convenient to expend much labor on buildings.

(*E.*) Nurseries should be made at the outset, for plants to put out in the second season. If three bushels are put in, the out-turn of plants ought to be 2 lacs. For the first year's planting, the plants will have to be purchased or otherwise procured, of plants produced from seed of the previous year. These are generally procurable in Wynaad at from 5 to 10 Rupees per 1,000.

If the plants are larger, they are better "stumped."

(*F.*) For roads or bridle paths 4 feet in the solid, the usual contract rate is Rupees 120 per mile.

(*G.*) "Lining" should be 6 feet between each row of plants, and 5 feet between each plant in the same row, this will make 1,452 plants per acre.

(*H.*) In Bamboo clearings where the second growth is very rapid and luxuriant, this work is arduous and expensive, and will usually cost fully 6 Rupees an acre; but in forest land after a good burn, Rupees 3 or less will probably cover the weeding expenses in the 1st year.

SECOND YEAR, *October 1st to September 30th.*

                                              RS. A. P.   RS. A. P.

Weeding the 50 acres planted in the
   1st year.............................. A 900 0 0

Filling up failures, 10 per cent.
  on 72,600 :

                                      RS. A. P.

Opening the pits, @ 40 for 4 As...45 6 0
Re-filling do.   120 at 4 As... 15 2 0
Planting do.   200 at 4 As... 9 0 0
                                        ———B 69 8 0

	RS.	A.	P.	RS.	A.	P.
Thatching and repairing buildings...	150	0	0			
Temporary bungalow.....................	300	0	0			
Repairing roads...........................	50	0	0			
Nurseries....................................	192	0	0			
				1,661	8	0
Felling and clearing 50 acres.........	1,000	0	0			
Lining and cutting pickets.............	150	0	0			
Pitting 50 acres, at 1,452 pits per acre	907	8	0			
Filling in the same.......................	151	4	0			
Planting up the same....................	90	12	0			
Clearing up and 1st weeding..........	300	0	0			
Writer's pay, at Rs. 30 per mensem..	360	0	0			
Maistries' pay.............................	426	0	0			
				3,385	8	0
Contingencies.............................				504	12	0
Rupees...				5,551	12	0

(A.) Weeding on cleaned forest clearings is estimated in Ceylon at not usually more than 20s. per acre per annum, and, indeed, it sometimes costs less. The case is quite different, however, on bamboo estates, or chena land, in which it will be found difficult to keep the ground free of weed, even at my estimate of Rupees 18 per acre per annum.*

(B.) Ten per cent. of failures may appear a large number, but it will not be found an excessive calculation, when we consider the number of causes which prove fatal to young plants, especially in the first-year.

---

* This estimate is authenticated by several of the leading planters in Wynaad.

THIRD YEAR, *October 1st to September 30th.*

	RS.	A.	P.	RS.	A.	P.
Weeding 100 acres, same rate as before...............................	1,800	0	0			
Filling up failures, 10 per cent. on 50 acres........................	69	8	0			
Do. do. 5 per cent. on 50 acres...	34	12	0			
Thatching & repairing buildings.	300	0	0			
Repairing roads.......................	100	0	0			
Nursery..................................	250	0	0			
				2,554	4	0
Pulping house & store & pulpers.	1,450	0	0			
Gathering 10 tons or 2,000 bushels cherry, at 4 Annas per bushel..................................	500	0	0			
Curing the same, at 8 As. per cwt.	100	0	0			
Despatching do. to the Coast, at 10 As. per bushel Parchment.	625	0	0			
				2,675	0	0
Maistries' pay...........................	625	0	0			
Writer's pay.............................	420	0	0			
Purchase of tools......................	218	0	0			
				1,263	0	0
Felling, clearing, lining, pitting, and planting 50 acres, at same rates as formerly.................	2,299	0	0			
Clearing up and 1st weeding the same..	300	0	0			
				2,599	0	0
Contingencies...				909	0	0
			Rupees...	10,000	4	0

The estimate of 4 cwts. per acre, maiden crop, in the 3rd year, is, I think, moderate and fair, as cases have been known* of its exceeding double quantity; as, however, I am determined that my estimates may not mislead persons into being over-sanguine, I prefer a low figure.

FOURTH YEAR, *October 1st to September 30th.*

	RS.	A.	P.	RS.	A.	P.
Weeding 150 acres now planted....................................	2,700	0	0			
Filling up failures, 10 per cent. on 50 acres.........69 8						
Do. 5 per cent. on 100 acres...... ....69 8						
	139	0	0			
Thatching and repairing buildings...................................	300	0	0			
Permanent set of lines.............	750	0	0			
Superintendent's bungalow......	2,000	0	0			
Repairing and making roads.....	180	0	0			
Nurseries...............................	200	0	0			
				6,269	0	0
Gathering 6,000 bushels cherry coffee............................:.....	1,500	0	0			
Curing the same......................	300	0	0			
Despatching to the Coast..........	1,875	0	0			
				3,675	0	0

* One clearing in Ceylon under my management gave 9 cwts. per acre maiden crop in 1858. In Wynaad, in 1861-1862, a field on a friend's property yielded first crop of 13 cwts. per acre.

	RS.	A.	P.	RS.	A.	P.
Writer's pay and Storekeeper..	660	0	0			
Maistries' pay.......................	996	0	0			
				1,656	0	0
Felling, clearing, lining, pitting, filling, planting and weeding 50 acres, at the same rates as before, making in all 200 acres now under cultivation..				2,599	8	0
Medical expenses and contingencies..				1,420	0	0
			Rupees...	15,619	8	0

It will be observed that I have estimated the probable crop as being its second from the coffee planted in the first year at 8 cwts. per acre, and the maiden crop in every season's planting at 4 cwts.

FIFTH YEAR, *October 1st to September 30th.*

	RS.	A.	P.	RS.	A.	P.
Weeding 200 acres, same rate as before..............	3,600	0	0			
Filling up failures, do. ...	173	12	0			
Repairing buildings, &c...	500	0	0			
Do. roads...............	150	0	0			
Nursery........	100	0	0			
Pruning and handling 150 acres, at 10 Rs.......	1,500	0	0			
Do. 50 ,, at 3 Rs......	150	0	0			
				6,173	12	0

	RS.	A.	P.	RS.	A.	P.
Cattle-shed building......	300	0	0			
Purchase of 50 head of cattle, at Rs. 15............	750	0	0			
Keep of stock............	300	0	0			
				1,350	0	0
Gathering 1,000 cwts. crop, at Annas 3 Pie 4 per bushel................	2,083	5	4			
Curing 1,000 cwts., same rate as before...............	500	0	0			
Despatching, at 10 Annas per bushel Parchment....	3,125	0	0			
				5,708	5	4
Writers and Storekeeper..	660	0	0			
Maistries' pay...........	935	0	0			
Contingencies and Medical expenses................	1,482	0	0			
				3,077	0	0
			Forward Rupees..	16,309	1	4

Summary of Estimate for five years.

	RS.	A.	P.		RS.	A.	P.
To expenses of 1st year, as above	10,095	12	0	By value of 10 tons crop, 3rd year	5,600	0	0
,, ,, 2nd ,, ,, ,,	5,551	12	0	,, ,, 30 ,, ,, 4th ,,	16,800	0	0
,, ,, 3rd ,, ,, ,,	10,000	4	0	,, ,, 50 ,, ,, 5th ,,	28,000	0	0
,, ,, 4th ,, ,, ,,	15,619	8	0	,, Probable crop in the 6th year, and in future annually, 80 tons.	44,800	0	0
,, ,, 5th ,, ,, ,,	16,309	1	0				
,, Probable expenses of 6th year	16,000	0	0				
,, Superintendence, at 2,000 Rupees per annum	12,000	0	0				
,, Purchase of horse, keep of the same, tappal and waterman, 6 years	3,312	0	0				
Rupees	88,888	5	0				
Credit of the Estate, Rs.	6,311	11	0				
Rupees	95,200	0	0	Rupees	95,200	0	0

It will be observed that no allowance has been made in the above for Interest on the money expended, or, indeed, any item which would not actually come under the eye of the Superintendent. Up to the third year, as no return would come in, all money up to that date expended would be worth 12 per cent. per annum, and these rates would considerably augment the sum total of expenses.

At the end of six years, the estate in thoroughly good order, *i. e.*, perfectly free of weeds, all vacancies annually supplied, and well pruned, would, at the present valuation, be worth *at least* Rupees 500 per acre, or *Rs.* 100,000.

We thus find, that to plant and carefully cultivate for six years, two hundred acres of land, bringing the whole into full bearing, will cost about £9,000, against which outlay a return by the value of crops may be expected, of about £9,500. After this period, the probable working expenses, including Manager's salary, &c., will perhaps amount to £2,000 per annum, and the crop to 1,600 cwts.; but putting the crops at 7 cwts. an acre only, or 1,400 cwts., worth at 56 shillings per cwt. nett £3,920, we have an annual profit of £1,920.

I think the above figures will be found as nearly correct as any *estimate* can be, though, in the actual carrying out of the theories above given, some variations would, of course, be experienced; in some cases the difference might be in favor of the planter, in others, adverse; my object has not been to show that in ordinary cases the profits resulting from coffee cultivation " will be something fabulous,"* as actual experience has shewn, that much care, hard labour, and expense must be incurred before a handsome profit can be expected; and it not unfrequently happens that, notwithstanding all these advantages, estates yield little but anxiety and disappointment to their owners, owing to bad soil, an exposed situation, too great an elevation, or *want of labor.*

---

* Dr. Shortt.

Estimate

For the cost of purchasing 200 acres of land in Ceylon, and bringing it into full bearing of coffee, calculated on the basis of labourer's pay being 8d. per diem for men, 6d. per diem for women and children.

First Year, *October 1st to September 30th.*

	£	s.	d.	£	s.	d.
Purchase of 200 acres forest				400	0	0
Felling, burning, and clearing 50 acres at contract rate, £2-5 per acre	112	10	0			
Lining out 50 acres, at 5s. per acre	12	10	0			
Holing 72,600 holes, at 30 holes per 8d.	80	13	4			
Filling do. do. 120 do. do. 8d.	20	3	4			
Plants, 72,600, at 3s. per 1,000	10	18	0			
Planting, at 200 per 8d.	12	2	0			
Roads, one mile	12	0	0			
				260	16	8
Weeding during 7 months, 10s. per acre	25	0	0			
3 dozen *Axes*, 2 dozen *Bill-hooks*, 50 *Mamoties*, 50 *Crowbars*, 1 dozen *Grass-hooks*, 1 Grindstone	26	0	0			
Rice and tool-store, lines, and Conductor's house, all of temporary nature	45	0	0			
				96	0	0

	£	s.	d.	£	s.	d.
Maistries', Canganies' pay............	27	8	0			
Conductor's pay........................	36	0	0			
Medical expenses and contingencies.	82	1	0			
				145	9	0
				£902	5	8

SECOND YEAR.

	£	s.	d.	£	s.	d.
Weeding 50 acres, 12 months' contract..	50	0	0			
Filling up vacancies by failures.....	9	4	8			
Thatching and repairing lines, &c..	10	0	0			
Repairing roads.........................	5	0	0			
Draining...................................	7	10	0			
				81	14	8
Felling, burning, and clearing 50 acres......................................	112	10	0			
Lining out 50 acres, at 5s. per acre..	12	10	0			
Holing 72,600 holes, at 30 holes per 8d....................................	80	13	4			
Filling do. at 120 do. 8d.	20	3	4			
Plants.......................................	10	18	0			
Planting at 200, 8d...................	12	2	0			
Roads, one mile.........................	12	0	0			
Weeding 50 acres new to 30th Sept.	25	0	0			
				286	16	8

	£	s.	d.	£	s.	d.
Canganies' pay.........	34	3	9			
Conductor's pay....	36	0	0			
Medical expenses and contingencies	41	6	0			
				111	9	9
				£480	1	1

Third Year.

	£	s.	d.	£	s.	d.
Weeding 100 acres, at £1 per acre	100	0	0			
Filling up vacancies....................	13	17	0			
New set of lines for coolies..........	50	0	0			
Reparing old do.	6	0	0			
Repairing roads and draining........	20	0	0			
Topping and handling 100 acres......	25	0	0			
				214	17	0
Purchase of new tools..................	18	0	0			
Contract for pulping house, store and pulpers—(buildings temporary).......	150	0	0			
Gathering 200 cwts. crop at 8d. per bushel.............	66	13	4			
Curing do. 10d. per cwt...	8	6	8			
Despatch do. to Colombo.....	41	13	4			
				284	13	4
Felling, burning, clearing, lining, holing, filling, plants, planting, weeding and roads for 50 acres, former rates.....................				286	16	8

	£	s.	d.	£	s.	d.
Conductor's pay	48	0	0			
Canganies' wages	65	0	0			
				113	0	0
Medical expenses and contingencies				90	16	0
				£990	2	0

Fourth Year.

	£	s.	d.	£	s.	d.
Weeding 150 acres, at £1 per acre	150	0	0			
Filling up vacancies	18	9	4			
Thatching and repairing buildings	25	0	0			
Superintendent's bungalow	200	0	0			
Repairing and making roads	25	0	0			
Gathering 600 cwts. of crop at 6d. per bushel	150	0	0			
Curing 600 do.	25	0	0			
Despatch do. to Colombo	125	0	0			
Mats and bags	55	0	0			
Pruning and handling	77	0	0			
				850	9	4
Felling, burning, clearing, lining, holing, filling, plants, planting, weeding, and roads for 50 acres, at former rates. This makes up 200 acres				286	16	8
Canganies' and Conductor's wages	116	10	0			
Medical expenses and contingencies	118	8	0			
				235	2	0
				£1,372	8	0

Fifth Year.

	£	s.	d.	£	s.	d.
Weeding 200 acres, at £1	200	0	0			
Filling up vacancies	23	1	8			
Thatching and repairing buildings	30	0	0			
Repairing roads and draining	50	0	0			
Handling and pruning	115	0	0			
Purchase of cattle, 75 head at 25s	93	15	0			
Building cattle-shed	50	0	0			
Keep of stock	36	0	0			
				597	16	8
Gathering 1,000 cwts. coffee at 6d. per bushel	250	0	0			
Curing do. do.	41	13	4			
Despatch to Colombo of the same	208	6	8			
1,000 bags, &c.	25	0	0			
				525	0	0
Canganies' and Conductor's wages	113	12	0			
Medical expenses and contingencies	121	6	0			
				234	18	0
				£1,357	14	8

Summary.

	£	s.	D.		£	s.	D.
To expenses of the 1st year	902	5	6	By crop in 3rd year	560	0	0
,, 2nd ,,	480	1	1	,, 4th ,,	1,680	0	0
,, 3rd ,,	990	2	0	,, 5th ,,	2,800	0	0
,, 4th ,,	1,372	8	0	,, Probable crop in the 6th year	3,920	0	0
,, 5th ,,	1,357	14	6	(or 200, 600, 1,000, and 1,400 cwts.)			
,, Probable outlay in the 6th year	1,500	0	0				
,, Purchase of a horse and keep, 6 years	256	0	0				
,, Waterman and tappals	144	0	0				
,, Superintendent's salary, 3 years £200, 2 at £250, 1 at £300	1,400	0	0				
£...	8,402	11	5				
Credit of Estate...	557	8	7				
£...	8,960	0	0		8,960	0	0

It will be noticed, in comparing the two estimates for Wynaad and Ceylon, that the cost of opening land in the former, slightly exceeds that in the latter, notwithstanding that the price of labour in Wynaad is only 4 annas (6*d*.) against 8*d*. in Ceylon. This is accounted for, by a great saving on several items, some of which I shall enumerate.

In the first place, I have not thought it advisable to put down more than £2 per acre as the cost of land, as an intending purchaser at a Government sale in Ceylon will seldom meet with much opposition from his brother-planters; and, indeed, late sales shew, that most of the blocks of land applied for, and sold during the past two years, have generally gone off, at the upset price of £1.

Felling, however, is entered at £2-5 for Ceylon, and £2 for Wynaad; in the former locality this work is always performed by contract at a fixed rate, in the latter by daily labour at 4 Annas per day; hence the difference.

With reference to "pitting," which is cheaper in Ceylon than in Wynaad, I can only say that my experience shews, that on an average, 20 pits (holes) is as much as can be got in the latter, as, during the long dry season which prevails every year, the ground becomes so exceedingly hard, that 15 or 16 is then the utmost coolies will make a day.

But in the matter of plants and nurseries, a very considerable saving is effected in Ceylon, inasmuch as any number of plants may, as I have before stated, be purchased from owners of small coffee gardens at from 3 to 5 per 1,000, whereas in Wynaad, either an expensive nursery must be formed, or plants purchased at various rates, varying between Rs. 5 and Rs. 10 per 1,000. It is, indeed, not uncommon for natives to form nurseries and withhold the sale of the plants until they have attained a good size, and then ask for them as much as Rupees 14 or Rupees 15 per 1,000.

Chiefly in the cost of *weeding*, however, does Ceylon appear most favorably, when placed in comparison with Wynaad. In the former, it is not at all unusual to keep young estates, commencing from the outset, perfectly clean, at 1s. or even less per acre, per month; many will be able to testify to this fact. In many cases Canganies will be found willing to contract to weed monthly at this rate. But in Wynaad, particularly in estates cleared in bamboo jungle, the grass weed and jungle spring up dense and luxuriantly the first season, and unless steadily and carefully repressed, increase in thickness every season; and I doubt if many estates are kept clean for the sum of Rs. 1-8 per acre per month, at which I have estimated.

The expense and difficulty of weeding in Wynaad is greatly increased by the continuous downpour of rain which takes place during the monsoon. During this season the rapidity of vegetation is astonishing, while it is difficult to check it, when the air is almost turned into water, and the ground into soft mud.

While considering this subject, I must not omit some notice of Dr. Shortt's estimates in the work he has recently brought out. Every one who has perused it and my own, cannot fail to be struck with the great difference between the estimates given in his, and those in the present work. As mine, however, are based on personal experience, I offer them to the public with great confidence, and I shall endeavour to shew some reasons why I thus openly impugn the correctness of those given by Dr. Shortt.

To any practical coffee cultivator, the task of judging of the authenticity of either will be an easy one, but the case would be quite different with a person who, ignorant of coffee matters, was still desirous of obtaining information on the subject, and who would naturally be puzzled on finding two such very conflicting statements brought out nearly at the same time, unless one author should boldly come forward and prove the correctness of his calculations.

There are other ways in which an excessively favourable and impossibly cheap estimate does much harm. Speculators, seeing such assertions as those Dr. Shortt puts forward, would be mortified and disappointed to find their hopes and expectations unrealized, as they assuredly would; and persons in England, or at a distance, who read that 200 acres of land may be purchased and converted into a coffee estate in one season for £716, would naturally look unfavourably on their Manager or Agent when they found under his auspices the real cost to be perhaps £1,600 or £1,700.

The following are the points in Dr. Shortt's estimates which I consider erroneous.

The sum of Rupees 5 per acre is certainly not sufficient to estimate as the price of land in Wynaad, as land cannot be now purchased at that price, unless subject to assessment, for which no allowance is made in the expenses of the two following years. Rupees 10 per acre is the *very minimum* for *felling*, but still this work *is* occasionally completed at that cost, but for " clearing, burning, &c.," we are indeed surprised to see Dr. Shortt put down so very moderate a sum as 8 Annas per acre; it would have been almost better not to have mentioned this item at all, and the omission might then have been attributed to an oversight; as the amount of brushwood left after a burn must indeed be small, if 2 men can lop, pile, and burn an acre in a day, and, in such case, where were the need of clearing it up at all. We might have supposed that Dr. Shortt alluded only to *forest* clearings, of which, with careful management, perhaps, 5 out of 10 burn so well as to obviate the necessity of any subsequent clearing up; but we are prevented from adopting this conclusion, by the remark which precedes the estimate, in which Dr. Shortt alludes to the difficulty of making a correct estimate, for general use, owing to the "difference of locality, soil, climate, command of labour, and also *the kind of land, whether forest, bamboo jungle, or otherwise,*" for all of which he says he makes allowance. Now, I can state, that out of three clearings in bamboo land felled in this season, which have come under my own observation, the one cost very nearly Rupees 10 per acre, one certainly Rupees 3 or Rupees 4, and the other between Rupees 5 to Rupees 6 per acre *for clearing up after the burning;* and I can state further, that bamboo land *seldom* burns so well as to cost less than Rupees 5 per acre, for clearing up subsequent to the burn, and I appeal to planters generally in support of my assertion.

With reference to forest clearings in Ceylon, an allowance of 15s. per acre is made for burning and clearing, in all cases where contracts are given for felling, burning, and clearing inclusive, on the chance of securing a good burn; and when, in order to save expense, planters have given the contract for *felling only*, most cases have resulted in an additional subsequent outlay, of even more than that sum for clearing up.

"Lining and marking out pits," cannot be done for Rupees 1·8 per acre, if this include cutting and pointing the pickets; Rupees 3 is much nearer the mark.

Fortunate, indeed, would be the planter who could get his land pitted at 5 Rupees per acre, *or for treble that sum*, and fortunate would he be, who in these days, could get 200 acres pitted up in one season *at any cost*. In remarking on the erroneousness of this estimate, we must not forget that Dr. Shortt inculcates making the pits 3 feet cube!

Every planter will agree with me when I say that 30 holes 18 inches cube is a good day's work for a coolie; at least, the Ceylon planters, who have a weakness for getting "a good day's work for a fair day's pay," think so, and so also do those in Wynaad. When 2-feet holes are required, 20, or even 15 to 18 in stony ground, are a good day's work. 30 holes 18 inches wide × 18 inches deep contain a space of 174,960 cubic inches: 18 at 2-feet cube contain 248,832 cubic inches. But we are informed by Dr. Shortt that coolies can make, "on an average, 35 pits 3 *feet wide and* 36 *inches deep*," or more than six times the amount of earthwork mentioned in the latter calculation, or nine times as much as what planters have generally hitherto been satisfied with, *i. e.*, 1,632,960 cubic inches.

Would not a boon be conferred on the planting world, if we were informed where such labourers could be found?

The Coorg planters had, I believe, within the last year or two, been giving 9 Rupees per 1,000 for pitting; at 6×5 feet planting, or 1,452 pits per acre, this amounts to about Rupees 13 per acre.

In Wynaad, Rupees 16 and even Rupees 18 per 1,000 have been ruling rates this year for contract work, this would be about Rupees 24 to Rupees 26 per acre; but Rupees 12 per 1,000 was formerly the usual rate, or Rupees 18 per acre; though one of the oldest planters about Manantoddy informed me that 10 years ago he gave as much as Rupees 20 per 1,000. The above are contract rates, which would necessarily be higher than the cost of work performed by daily labourers at 4 Annas per diem, and, calculating the cost at 25 pits for 4 Annas, the amount would be *Rupees* 14-8 per acre, and any one conversant with the present state of labour in the Madras Presidency would, doubtless, be well content that it should cost no more.

It will be observed that Dr. Shortt has made no allowance for weeding, in the expenses of the first year; this is an oversight which makes probably a difference of Rupees 1,200 less than the real cost. We have, therefore, on the three items above taken into consideration, a difference of, probably, say—

    On clearing................ Rs. 1,000
    On pitting................... „ 2,000
    And on weeding............. „ 1,200=Rs. 4,200

in all, most likely more, in the 1st year's expenses.

In the estimate for the 2nd year, we see Rs. 800 named as the cost of "12 monthly weedings" for 200 acres, this is

5 Annas 4 Pie per acre monthly, or Rupees 4 per annum. This is far lower than the cheapest weeding in Ceylon, where it is a source of pride to the planter to be able to keep his estate clean at £1 per acre per annum, and where it is indeed an extraordinary thing to be able to do so at 1 shilling per acre monthly : let us calculate the distance over which a coolie would have to go at this latter rate ; 1,000 trees, at 5 feet apart, or nearly a mile, carefully inspecting a space 2 yards wide, and picking out every weed he comes across, and we shall see that weeds in such a case must be few and far between. But when we recollect that Dr. Shortt has (as he says) made allowance for " difference of land, &c.," and knowing the growth of weeds in bamboo land, where the grass springs up as luxuriantly as in the richest European pasture, the inadequacy of the sum allowed appears the more extraordinary.

Take the average of the estates in North or South Wynaad ; what does the weeding cost ? and what would it cost were coolies plentiful enough to keep them clean ? (which is not always the case) *at least* 18 Rupees per annum per acre ; and this is good work.

I consider also Rs. 100 as allowed for cost of filling up vacancies, an insufficient estimate ; I have in my foregoing calculations given the detailed account of the probable cost of this work which, at the same rates on 200 acres, would amount to Rupees 278.

Thus, from what I have stated, I think it will at once be seen that Dr. Shortt's estimates are *not* applicable to Wynaad, or Ceylon. I have considered it my duty to prove this, in a work such as the present, in order that neither the public generally, nor proprietors of estates, should be misled as to an investment, which, though really highly remunerative, *if well conducted*, is not the El Dorado, which will yield a " fabulous" return for a very small outlay, or the exhibition of *a very limited knowledge* of the subject.

CHAPTER XXI.

Practical hints for the medical treatment of coolies and others on coffee estates until professional assistance can be obtained.

Medicines, &c., required.

Sulphate of Quinine.	Caustic.
Carbonate of Soda.	Blistering ointment.
Dover's Powders.	Mustard.
Calomel.	Turpentine.
Jalap.	Sugar of Lead.
Laudanum.	Rhubarb.
Ipecacuanha Powder.	Powdered Nitre.
Castor Oil.	Sulphur.
Epsom Salts.	Treacle.
Cholera Drops.	A syringe.
Essence of Peppermint.	

FEVER.

" For ordinary attacks, give half a tea spoonful of Jalap, a tea spoonful of Salts, and about ⅓ of a tea spoonful of Quinine (in powder, not lump) mixed together in a wine glassful of water, with a few drops of Essence of Peppermint if at hand. If this does not act on the bowels in four hours, repeat the dose, slightly diminished. This dose will often cure fever in natives, but in Europeans it should be followed by Quinine—say ½ of a tea spoonful of powdered

Quinine 2 or 3 times a day, dissolved in a wine glassful of water, beginning as soon as the above-mentioned purgative has done its work.

If the taste of the Quinine be disliked, make it into pills, 3 or 4 grains each, with a little bread crumb or boiled rice.

Persons in charge of large bodies of coolies should keep these medicines made up ready for use, thus—

Purgative Mixture.

2 Dessert spoonsful of Jalap,

2 Table spoonsful of Epsom Salts,

2 Tea spoonsful of Quinine powder, and a few drops of Essence of Peppermint in a wine bottle of water.

Dose.—A wine glassful of the above to be repeated in four hours, if the first has not operated.

Quinine Mixture.

40 Grains (*i. e.*, 2 scruples, or about 2 tea spoonsful of Quinine Powder, and a little essence of Peppermint in a wine bottle of water.

Dose.—A wine glassful.

One such dose will cure or prevent fever returning; if not, continue it two or three times a day.

Each European should have a bottle of Warburg's Fever Tincture, and take it according to the printed instructions on the bottle.

If there be much shivering and headache, at the commencing of the attack, an emetic of half a tea spoonful, of Ipecacuanha powder, or one tea spoonful of mustard in water, will afford relief. Promote the vomiting by large draughts of warm water. In such case the stomach should be allowed to settle, before the purgative is taken. If headache continue bad, or dilirium or contusion of thought come on, apply a blister, (or mustard plaster) to the back of the neck."

(The above is by *Dr. Elliott, taken from Ferguson's Common-Place Book.*)

D'Esterre's Fever Powders will be found very efficacious and easy of use, they should be administered according to the instructions printed on each packet, after the action of the purgative mixture above.

It is sometimes thought better in using Quinine, to commence with large doses of from 8 to 10 grains, to an adult, decreasing the dose gradually to 2 or 3 grains.

Another mixture which I have used with the utmost success in treating coolies, is the prescription of a very clever medical friend of mine, *i. e.*,

    2 scruples Quinine,
    2 drachms Powdered Nitre,
    1½ Wine glassful of Brandy, in a wine bottle of water.

DOSE.—One wine glassful 3 times a day after the action of the purgative.

As soon as the fever has ceased, nourishment should be taken, as the exhaustion which follows an attack is very great. Owing to their inability to procure nourishing food at this period, coolies frequently fall into a state of great weakness, and are then very liable to be attacked by Dropsy; for the cure of this complaint I recommend the following, having administered it with great success:—

    1 oz. Flour of Sulphur,
    2 drachms Powdered Nitre,
    2 scruples Quinine, in a wine bottle of Treacle.

DOSE.—1 Wine glassful twice a day.

While the patient is taking this medicine, he should be fed with broth, or other nourishing diet, and half a glass of Brandy or Arrack, daily.

BOWEL COMPLAINT.

" Do not allow the bowels to be more than 3 or 4 times purged in one day without taking 20 or 30 drops of Laudanum in a little water. If that be not sufficient, take as much Dover's Powder as will go on a 3*d*. piece and as much Quinine as will go on a 6*d*. piece, two or three times a day. Avoid salt meat, and take *white* bread, rice, broth, tea, &c."—*Dr. Elliott, taken from Ferguson's Common-Place Book.*

As Diarrhœa frequently proceeds solely from a disordered stomach, it will be well, after the Laudanum has stopped it, to take a small dose of Castor oil, which will prevent a recurrence of the attack.

If no medicine be at hand, a little powdered chalk, or powder of burnt cork in a wine glass of brandy and water, will sometimes stop the attack.

DYSENTERY.

" If there be much pain, or twisting in the bowels, with blood and mucus in the motions with straining, it is Dysentery. Take the same powders. 1 Dover's to cover a 3*d*. piece, and Quinine to cover a 6*d*. piece every 4, 5 or 6 hours, according to the urgency of the symptoms.

" These Diarrhœa and Dysentery powders should be kept ready made up, and in good quantity, where there are gangs of men employed—that is, 5 grains of Dover's Powder and 3 grains of Quinine in each powder, folded in paper, and kept in a wide mouthed bottle."

" If there be much straining at stool, give $\frac{1}{2}$ a tea spoonful of laudanum in ½ a wine glassful of cold water, as an injection with a small syringe: and repeat it, if necessary, 2 or 3 times a day.

"In Europeans, passing much blood, with pains and fever, apply 12 or 18 leeches in the *early* stages, over the most painful parts. Fine leeches can be got in the paddy-fields. Take a hip bath, by sitting in a small tub of hot water twice a day: and keep hot clay or sand in a pillow case spread upon the belly.

"Diminish the medicines *gradually*, that is, from 4 to 3 times to twice, and to once a day: for if given up suddenly, the disease will probably return.

"Take only farinaceous food, such as *white* bread, arrow-root, &c., and broth (without vegetables), as improvement takes place." *Dr. Elliott.*

In many cases, if the complaint be taken early especially, nothing will be found more efficacious than Dr. Collis Browne's Chlorodyne, in both Diarrhœa and Dysentery, or in Cholera.

Another remedy for Dysentery, not very much known, is as follows :—

Apply a mustard plaster for 15 or 20 minutes to the stomach, and then administer 30 grains of Ipecacuanha Powder, *made into Pills:* this should be taken without liquid, or it will act as an emetic; if kept down, it will be found to exert a wonderful effect. The dose should be repeated 3 times a day as long as is necessary.

Cholera.

"Be provided with 'Cholera Drops' or 'mixture,' to be had at the Druggists, and which is usually composed of various aromatics, with Opium, and use according to the instructions.

"Or give Laudanum 20 to 30 drops, with a tea spoonful or two of Brandy, a little Carbonate of Soda, sugar, and any spices you may have, *in hot water*, every 1, 2 or 3 hours, according to the emergency, until vomiting or purging is relieved.

"Intense vomiting may often be stopped by a tea spoonful of Carbonate of Soda dissolved in hot water, and *drunk as hot as possible*. If thrown up, repeat the dose.

"Lay a large mustard poultice on the stomach for 10 or 15 minutes.

"Pills made of Calomel, Camphor, and Morphine, have been found very efficacious. They are retained in the stomach when fluid medicines are rejected. The pill should consist of two grains Calomel, three grains Camphor, and a quarter of a grain of Morphine. A pill should be taken every 3 or 4 hours, until purging and vomiting subside, and the heat of the body is restored."

"During the prevalence of an epidemic, every effort should made to check the premonitory Diarrhœa: 30 drops of Laudanum in hot Brandy and water, will be found very efficacious." (*Dr. Elliott.*)

In addition to the above remedies, it will be advisable to apply hot bottles to the feet, thighs, and arm-pits, and to rub the limbs strongly to restore and keep up circulation. A hot bath of mustard and water may also be resorted to if practicable.

LIVER.

"Stitch or pain about the right side without purging, is

probably the beginning of inflammatiom of the liver. Purge freely with Jalap, Castor oil, or Salts, or the purging mixture given above for fever. Give Quinine (as much as will go on a six-pence) 3 or 4 times a day. Foment the side, or apply the hot sand as above. If a strong or newly arrived European, apply 1 or 2 dozen leeches. Live low, and carefully avoid all strong drink, Wine, Beer, &c." (*Dr. Elliott.*)

SNAKE BITES.

Pinch up the skin between the finger and thumb, and cut out a piece about the size of a shilling. Be sure you cut out the scratch made by *both* fangs of the snake. If you cannot pinch up the skin, stick a pin or anything else to lift it up, but in any way cut or dig out the piece. Any knife whether pen or table-knife will answer. Have no fear of the consequences of your cut; there is no artery near the surface that you need be apprehensive of pening. A bandage will therefore stop any bleeding which may follow. Cut, however late, and cut bloody, for life often depends on your doing so. *Dr. Elliott.*

Another and curious remedy, much recommended of late years, is as follows :—Run the blade of a pen-knife or lancet through the part bitten, in two cuts transversely, and immediately rub into the wound thus made, some Ipecacuanha powder.

A red hot iron immediately applied to the part, is a safe and expeditious cure; it is more quickly done than using the knife, to which the patient will frequently make much resistance.

If the bite is on the hand or foot, tie a ligature round

the limb above the part as lightly as possible, to prevent the circulation of the venom. A glass of Brandy will be of use to stimulate the system to resist the action of the poison.

Cuts and Wounds.

"Wash out any dirt, and bind up but not too tightly, and after a day or two begin to wet with cold water. Dress afterwards with folded cloth, kept wet with cold water, or water with a little sugar of lead in it, laying over all a plantain or other large leaf, to keep the part moist.

"Keep well covered to prevent flies from getting in and breeding maggots, as they so do in this country. If the wound becomes painful, the probability is, there are maggots in it; in which case, put in calomel, which will kill them, without irritating the wound. If you have no calomel, use tobacco and Datura Stramonium pounded together.

The Datura is called, in Singhalese " Atthenna," and in Tamil " Woomoothoo," and grows almost every where." *Dr. Elliott.*

When much inflammation appears in the neighbourhood of the wound, and the cold water and sugar of lead appears insufficient, to reduce it, lay on it a cloth kept wet with Brandy, one part; vinegar, two parts; cold water, four parts.

For gunpowder wounds, where the flesh is much torn and burnt, bathe the part, for a short time in warm water, and then wash it carefully with the same; then apply a warm poultice of oatmeal porridge as often as necessary for a few days. Then make a lotion of sweet oil, and chunam well mixed together to the consistency of custard, and apply to the part with a feather, or a piece of muslin laid on and a light bandage over it.

Fractures and Dislocations.

Put the limb into the easiest position, and send for surgical assistance. Keep down inflammation with cold water applied to the part, or brandy, vinegar and cold water, as above recommended. If the patient be likely to faint or become exhausted, give a little brandy and a few grains of quinine.

Sores.

Coolies are very liable to bad sores, principally on the legs, produced by festered scratches, &c. If the sore be large, foul, and unhealthy, wash carefully with warm water and soap, then apply soft warm poultices for a few days, until its appearance becomes more clean and active. After this a lotion, composed of bluestone, 2 drachms, or sulphate of zinc, 2 drachms, to a wine bottleful of cold water may be applied on a clean piece of thin, old linen, to be kept continually wet.

When the "proud flesh" has become diminished, and the sore shews symptoms of drying up, Turner's Cerate used on lint, a fresh dressing every morning and evening.

FINIS.